WE KNEW MATT TALBOT

# We knew Matt Talbot

## VISITS WITH HIS RELATIVES
## AND FRIENDS

*by*

REV. ALBERT H. DOLAN

*Order of Carmelites*

THE CARMELITE PRESS

55 Demarest Avenue
Englewood, New Jersey

6413 Dante Avenue
Chicago 37, Illinois

# CONTENTS

# LIST OF ILLUSTRATIONS

*Most of the pictures in this book were taken by Father Ronald Gray, O. Carm.; some few by Father Dolan; the others by Charles Fennell of the Dublin *Standard*.

# FOREWORD

OUR journey to Ireland was a flight to a Catholic wonderland, in which we met many who, by reason of their association with Matt Talbot, are submerged in a cause bigger than the world and as lasting as eternity. Hence I am privileged to express here my joy at having accompanied Father Dolan on the pilgrimage to Dublin recorded in this book; likewise am I blessed in having met personally the men and women whose consuming devotion to the holy penitent, Matt Talbot, could be the spark that will ignite in America universal enthusiasm for Dublin's favorite son. Because of previous connections, Father Dolan was alone during his visit to Sir Joseph Glynn and the Dublin Carmel; I was, however, fortunate to be present when he interviewed all the other friends and relatives of Matt Talbot.

Naturally I listened attentively while Father Dolan questioned the shy and deeply religious friends of "poor holy Matt." Whether sitting in a living room or merely standing in a dim alley-way, I absorbed eagerly all the edifying and illuminating information that the charming associates of Matt communicated to us.

As I read the story of our pilgrimage, so vividly told in these pages, I re-lived our journey and marvelled at the complete exactness with which those conversations are reproduced here. This exactness was achieved by painstaking transcription of notes Father Dolan jotted down during each conversation.

I completely agree with Father Dolan that the holiness of Matt Talbot seems to have overflowed into the circle of his living associates, and no one could meet the friends and relatives of Matt Talbot without being better for the experience and without conceiving a deep appreciation of his holiness.

It is an honor for me to introduce you to these friends of ours; may they become your life-long friends, because they mirror perfectly the holiness of Matt Talbot. If your new-found friends, the friends of Matt Talbot, affect you as they have affected us, then the spirit of Matt's holiness, having overflowed from them into you, will continue its onward sweep and will eventually deluge the world with a love of God which was the basis and the source of the penitential life of Ireland's workingman, Matt Talbot.

RONALD F. GRAY, O. CARM.

*December 8, 1947*

# PRAYER FOR THE CANONIZATION OF
## MATTHEW TALBOT

O Jesus, true friend of the humble penitent, Who hast given us in Thy servant, Matthew, a wonderful example of victory over vice, a model of penance and of love for Thy Holy Eucharist, grant, we beseech Thee, that we Thy servants may overcome all our wicked passions and sanctify our lives with penance and love like his.

And if it be in accordance with Thy adorable designs that Thy pious servant should be glorified by the Church, deign to manifest by Thy heavenly favours the power he enjoys in Thy sight, Who livest and reignest for ever and ever. Amen.

*(The above prayer, issued and approved by the Archbishop of Dublin, carries with it an indulgence of 100 days for each recitation.)*

# 1.

## *Matt Talbot; The Matt Talbot Legion*

MATT TALBOT was born in Dublin, Ireland, in 1856. At the age of twelve he left school and at that tender age became a drunkard. Thereafter for sixteen years he was drunk at every opportunity. When he was twenty-eight years old, he took a pledge of total abstinence, which he never broke. During those forty-one years between his pledge and his death in 1925, he not only remained a total abstainer, but also achieved a holiness which is duplicated only in the lives of the greatest saints.

But lest any reader should imagine that his victory was easy, let us watch him as he fought the drink fiend in his blood. Matt found the initial battle all but overwhelming. The habits of sixteen years were arrayed against him; his nerves, deprived of their accustomed soothing draughts, screamed their protests. Moreover, after so many years of neglect of prayer, the effort to pray was wearisome in the extreme. But when prayer was most difficult, he prayed for the grace to be able to pray.

Every evening, every Saturday afternoon, and all day Sunday, except at meal-time, he spent in church trying to pray. Those hours in church were deadly. He simply knelt there, weary, cold, dispirited, unnerved . . . but holding on. Returning home at night discouraged and disheartened, he would say to his mother, "I fear it's no use, Mother. I'll drink again when the three months are up." His mother encouraged him, effectively, and he continued to fight his battle in the company of Christ and with one weapon: prayer. When the three months expired he renewed his pledge of total abstinence for a year. At the end of the year, he took the pledge for life, and kept it perfectly. He was twenty-

1

eight; the fury of the battle against liquor was largely over; the rest of his story is one of growth in holiness.

The life of prayer, which Matt commenced on the day of his first pledge, he continued with increasing fervor until his death. I know of no living person, lay or cleric, who gives as much time daily to prayer as Matt did. Of every twenty-four hours he devoted ten hours to prayer. In short, he gave to prayer *all* his non-working hours. Is it strange that he who had given all his free time to drink, should after his conversion give all his free time to prayer? Doubtless he asked himself, "Shall I be less generous in giving my time to my Friend in the Tabernacle than I was in giving my time to my friends in the tavern?"

His service of his Master did not by any means end with prayer. His life was one of service to his fellow-man. He lived on $1.20 a week and gave away the rest of his salary to charity. He was no eccentric hermit but a lovable, warmly human person, who loved children and animals and who maintained relations of the most fragrant charity with his relatives, friends and fellow-laborers. "His fellow-workmen," says one witness, "loved Matt Talbot."

Matt resolved to replace his years of self-indulgence with years of self-discipline. He distrusted his once rebellious body and its appetites, and therefore determined to keep every appetite, whether for food or sleep or comfort, under complete control. He had been the slave of his body; he would now make the body his slave.

Accordingly he curtailed his sleep to three and one-half hours daily. He slept on an iron bed with planks for a mattress. He undertook prolonged and severe fasting. He did not parade these fasts but concealed them from all but the members of his immediate family. Fourteen years before he died he had become so accustomed to these penances that he felt bound to undertake another penance. He wound iron chains tightly about his legs and arms, under his clothes, next his skin. This secret he kept from all. He was a man of iron, with a heart of gold, and into his generous being was packed all that is noblest in Christian spirituality.

On June 6, 1925, this sixty-nine year old laborer completed his last day's work. The next day, Sunday, June 7,

*Above.* The Customs House, Dublin, where Matt worked for his father, who had charge of the whiskey stores bonded in the Customs House. *Right.* Bob Talbot, Matt's youngest brother. Bob died in his thirties, but resembled Matt when the latter was thirty. *Below left.* Mr. William Powell, who worked with Matt Talbot at Martin's. See page 32. *Below right.* Mrs. Anne Keogh, who came to Matt when he fell dying in Granby Lane. See page 124.

while on his way to Mass, he suffered a heart attack and dropped dead in a street near his home. In the morgue, while his body was being prepared for burial, a Sister of Mercy found his chains. His secret was out. The discovery of the chains on his body led to an inquiry into his life and soon his holiness became known. It was not until he was dead that people began to know how he had lived.

His story became known almost over-night, and soon his humble grave in Glasnevin Cemetery became a place of pilgrimage, and today literally millions pray that Rome will eventually declare him a saint.

### The Matt Talbot Legion

Early in 1947 when word reached America that Matt Talbot's Cause for beatification had been introduced in Rome, I hurriedly completed the first American life of Matt Talbot, which I had been preparing for several years. The life was entitled *Matt Talbot, Alcoholic.* The enthusiastic reception accorded the book confirmed our belief that the time was ripe for a movement, under Catholic auspices, to help alcoholics, the number of whom was and is alarmingly increasing throughout the United States.

Accordingly our Father Provincial, the Very Reverend Matthew T. O'Neill, O. Carm., and his Provincial Council decided to launch, without any further delay, "The Matt Talbot Legion," which was to be a movement of prayer and education to aid alcoholics, under the sponsorship of the Carmelite Order. Our newly elected Prior General, the Most Reverend Kilian Lynch, O. Carm., gave his approval.

It was further decided that the Legion should have as its patrons not only Matt Talbot but also the Holy Ghost, Our Lady, the refuge of sinners, and St. Therese of Lisieux, to whom Matt Talbot was so devoted and who promised to "spend her heaven doing good upon earth."

This year of 1947 being the Golden Jubilee Year of St. Therese, our Father Provincial asked me and Father Ronald Gray, O. Carm., the Assistant Director of The Matt Talbot Legion, to go to Dublin by way of Lisieux to place the beginnings of The Matt Talbot Legion under her protection.

Father Ronald and I arrived in Lisieux in August of this year, 1947, and after imploring the Little Flower's intercession in favor of the project and asking her living sisters to pray for its success, we set out for Dublin.*

Our duties there, as outlined by our Superiors, were to visit the places sanctified by Matt Talbot and to interview any persons still living who knew him, and to procure, if possible, some Relics of Matt Talbot to be placed at the National Offices of The Matt Talbot Legion in Englewood, N. J.

It should be said here that just as we Americans honor the relics of our heroes, just as we preserve and venerate the home of Washington, the sword of Grant and the pen of Lincoln, so the Catholic Church preserves and honors the relics of its heroes. The only difference is that God sometimes bestows, through the Relics of the Saints, wonderful favors and graces.

We foresaw that the assignment of procuring Relics would not be easy of execution, first because we knew that all the members of Matt Talbot's immediate family were dead, his two sisters having died in 1934 and 1941 respectively; and secondly, because we feared that his Relics had been commandeered by the Archbishop of Dublin when the diocesan process of inquiry was inaugurated.

However, before we left America, Cardinal Spellman, at my request, gave me a letter of introduction to Archbishop McQuaid of Dublin, and we had confided to St. Therese and Matt Talbot himself the success of the journey. Throughout our sojourn in Dublin, we could almost feel them both at our side and I think the reader will also sense their presence and guidance as the story of the visit unfolds.

*For the story of his visits with the sisters of St. Therese, see Father Dolan's *The Sisters of St. Therese Today*, Carmelite Press.

# 2.

# *Visit to Granby Lane and Glasnevin;*
# *Mrs. Purcell*

WE arrived in Dublin at midnight on Saturday, August 16.
The next morning, Sunday, after Mass, Father Ronald and
I went first to kneel at the spot in Granby Lane where Matt
Talbot dropped dead June 7, 1925 on his way to Mass. A
cross marks the spot in the Lane where he died and a little
shrine to him has been erected there (see photograph on
page 9) on which fresh flowers are placed daily by a Mrs.
Purcell whose acquaintance I was soon to make. After a
prayer at his shrine, I noticed a little religious shop a few
steps away. In its show window my eye first fell on an Irish
Catholic Truth Society pamphlet entitled *The Friends of
St. Therese of Lisieux!* Happy omen. I entered and was
met by the owner of the shop, Mrs. Susan Purcell. A few
minutes conversation with her revealed her deep devotion
to Matt, and to St. Therese as well.

I asked, "Do many come here to Granby Lane?"

She replied, "All day long every day in the year there
is a steady stream of pilgrims, especially during these summer months." I was in Granby Lane several times each day
thereafter, and the Lane was never without its devotees of
Matt Talbot piously visiting his shrine for the first time.
Mrs. Purcell showed me the register in which she asked
visitors to sign their names. There were there the names of
prelates, priests and lay people from every country under
the sun.

"What about the people of Dublin, Mrs. Purcell?" I
asked. "Do they come here too?"

"There are some," she replied, "who come every morning or evening for nine days for a private novena to him. Others come every day of the year."

While I was still looking over the register, Mrs. Purcell said, "Will you sign the register, Father? And may I ask your name?"

"My name is Father Dolan, a Carmelite from America."

"Not Father Albert Dolan?" she said excitedly. I assured her that was the name.

"Why, you're no stranger to me, Father. I've read all your Little Flower books!"

I had indeed found a friend. There was no one in Dublin, not even the Archbishop, who was as helpful to me in achieving my objectives as Mrs. Purcell. She had known intimately Matt Talbot's two sisters; she knew nearly everyone, especially women, who still lived who had known Matt Talbot and, besides, she knew their addresses. Moreover she had the most precious Relics of Matt Talbot, which she proudly showed me that first morning: one of his books, his *Life of Christ* by Fouard, two sheets of Matt's own handwriting, and portions of Matt's woolen sock and cotton blanket. On one of the two sheets he had made a list, as his job of storeman in the lumber yard required, of lumber requisitioned from him on a particular day. On the other sheet, he had copied a passage from one of those religious books he was in the habit of borrowing for his spiritual reading.

"You are indeed rich," I said to Mrs. Purcell. "Almost too rich." She looked at me questioningly as if she expected me to say more. But that was all that morning. We'll meet Mrs. Purcell again and often in these pages.

"I'll return later," I said, "I have to go now because I want to visit Matt's grave at noon when the crowds are there."

I knew from a clipping from the Dublin "Standard" which a friend in Ireland had sent me, that every Sunday of the year at noon, about a hundred members of the Legion of Mary gather at Matt's grave in Glasnevin Cemetery to recite the Rosary and the Prayer for Matt's Canonization. "Never once in the last dozen years," says the *Standard*, "has this act of devotion been omitted."

In planning to be at the cemetery at noon, I had not reckoned on the almost universal egress of the people of Dublin that hot summer Sunday to the seashore and on the consequent difficulty in finding a taxi. We arrived at the grave just as the pilgrims were dispersing after their prayers.

Father Dolan kneeling at Matt Talbot's grave.

The humble workingman, Matt Talbot, has no such imposing monument, of course, as O'Connell and thousands of other Irish heroes in Glasnevin. It is a simple grave on the very farthest edge of the cemetery. It is surmounted by a Celtic Cross in the center of which is carved the Sacred Heart. The slab bears the inscription: "Sacred to the Memory of Matt Talbot who died June 7, 1925, aged 69. This monument has been erected by the members of the Sodality of Our Lady Immaculate of St. Francis Xavier's Church, Upper Gardiner Street, of which he was a fervent member for 40 years." (See the photograph above).

As I knelt at the grave in prayer, I opened my eyes and there on the earth of the grave was a medallion of St. Therese! I inquired later of Mrs. Purcell why some one had left it there and she explained that such medals are often left there by the Irish people to remind Matt, as it were, of their petition to him.

Father Ronald kneeling before Matt's shrine in Granby Lane. Note the fresh flowers, daily renewed by Mrs. Purcell.

When I returned to my hotel in the early afternoon, there was a note from Mrs. Purcell in which she said, "I am hoping that in America you can do for our Matt what you did for our St. Therese. I love them both. I pledge myself to help you in every way possible and will consider it an honor to work hand in hand with the American Apostle of St. Therese." Her help was invaluable and "our" St. Therese was everywhere in evidence throughout our work in Dublin.

# 3.

## Visit With Sir Joseph Glynn

THAT first Sunday afternoon, I went to the Sacred Heart Convent to visit Mother Connelly, the Superior, with whom I had been in correspondence concerning Matt Talbot for several months before leaving America. I had mailed to her a list of questions about him: who now possessed Matt's books; where were his famous iron bed and wooden pillow; what relatives of his were still living; who had the papers found in his room after his death on which he had copied in his own hand passages from books he had read; were any of the laborers who had worked with him in the lumber yard still living; was Sir Joseph Glynn, his first biographer, still alive and if so, where? I had asked her to compile answers to those questions before I arrived in Dublin. Upon my arrival at the convent, Mother Connelly told me that she had forwarded my questions to the very much alive Sir Joseph Glynn, of whom she had been a friend since their childhood. She telephoned Sir Joseph of my arrival and he was kind enough to invite me to visit him immediately.

I spent the rest of the afternoon with Sir Joseph who was the first to make Matt Talbot known to the world and who knows more about Matt than any other living man. Sir Joseph is a completely charming gentleman, now seventy-eight years of age. He lives with his wife in a palatial home on Ailesbury Road in Dublin. He is stone-blind but his faculties are alert and his memory unimpaired. He retains his chairmanship of several large Dublin corporations.

After exchanging greetings, I said, "It is an honor, Sir Joseph, to meet the man who gave Matt Talbot to the world."

"It is a pleasure to meet the first American biographer of Matt," he replied. "I congratulate you upon your book

*Matt Talbot, Alcoholic.* It is a new approach, a fresh presentation instead of a rehash of the familiar story. I like its plan and division and its adherence to one theme. I am one of the chairmen of the Catholic Truth Society of Ireland, and I would like to publish an Irish edition of your book. With that in view, would you permit me to make an appointment for you to meet Doctor O'Reilly, Executive Secretary of the Catholic Truth Society of Ireland?"

Of course I agreed, and later in the week met Doctor O'Reilly at Veritas House, Lower Abbey Street. It was arranged that they publish later an Irish edition of *Matt Talbot, Alcoholic.*

Sir Joseph then took from his pocket my letter to Mother Connelly and said, "Your coming here saves me from writing a long letter in answer to your questions which Mother Connelly forwarded to me. I'd much rather answer them orally."

"I have a much longer list of questions here, Sir Joseph, and if you don't mind, I'll put the questions and write out your answers." He agreed.

"How," I inquired, "did you happen to interest yourself in Matt Talbot in the first place and write his life so soon after his death?"

"Matt," he answered, "was entirely unknown to me until a friend of mine who had known Matt for twenty-six years told me of him and suggested that I write his life."

"Who was that friend?"

"His name was Raphael O'Callaghan. He was the gentleman from whose library Matt used to borrow religious books. He knew Matt as well as or better than anyone else. It was less than a month after Matt's death that Raphael suggested that I write his life. I told him that I would not dare put pen to paper without witnesses. Raphael replied, 'I'll get you all the witnesses you want'; and he did. I had the book ready for publication in December, 1925, seven months after Matt's death, but it was not published until March of the next year."

I inquired about its circulation and Sir Joseph replied, "The Irish edition now exceeds 350,000 copies and there are translations of it into French, German, Dutch, Portu-

Father Dolan with Archbishop McQuaid, Archbishop of Dublin and Primate of Ireland.

guese, Spanish, Hungarian, Czech, Polish, Italian, Russian, and other languages—twenty-one in all."

As he talked, Sir Joseph inadvertently took from his lower vest pocket what looked like a Relic and was fingering it as he talked. I asked, "Is that a Relic of Matt Talbot?"

"No," he said, "that's a Relic of the Little Flower!"

Ever present St. Therese, I thought. At the grave, with Mrs. Purcell, and now here with Sir Joseph. She was, although I did not know it then, to make other similar appearances later during those Dublin days.

Sir Joseph continued, "I've treasured her Relic for many years. Like yourself, I've been to Lisieux and therefore have been enjoying the story of your visits there, in your books, which Mother Connelly sent me and which my wife has been reading to me. How strange that we both should be so devoted both to Matt Talbot and to St. Therese."

I then explained to Sir Joseph my desire to interview personally all those still living who knew Matt Talbot, and asked their names and addresses.

"His two sisters," he replied, "who knew him best, Mrs. Mary Andrews and Mrs. Susan Fylan, are dead, as you know. He had a third sister who married and moved away and who knew nothing of him. I was able to get much information about his *early* life from Mrs. Andrews. After she married, she was for the most part out of touch with him. It was Mrs. Fylan who supplied me with data concerning his later years."

"Who is his nearest living relative now?"

"His sister's daughter; the daughter of Mrs. Andrews. Her name is Mrs. Byrne. Her son James applied to me recently for work and I'll look up the address for you." (He could not find it just then but Mrs. Purcell discovered it for me later and Mrs. Byrne was to play an important part in the success of my mission to Dublin.)

"Is Mrs. Manning, the lodgekeeper's wife, who used to prepare Matt's noon meal, still living?"

"Yes, I believe she is, and also her husband, and their children, who used to observe Matt at prayer in his 'office' in the timber yard and of whom Matt was so fond. I think you could get their address from Father O'Donnell, the Vice-Postulator of Matt's Cause." (Both Father O'Donnell and the Mannings were to loom large in my quest during the next few days.)

"Are there any others, not relatives, still living, who knew Matt?"

Sir Joseph mentioned the names of some of Matt's fellow workmen, especially Mr. Edward Carew, who were still in the employ of the firm for which Matt worked, the T. and C. Martin Lumber Company. I later found and interviewed all these men.

"Another man who knew Matt Talbot well is Brother Furlong, the porter at the Jesuit Church in Upper Gardiner Street. He will be able to tell you much of Matt if, as I think, he's still there. Then there is a Mrs. Sweeney, who was the custodian of Matt's room for ten years after his death. She knew both Matt's sisters well. She is the lady who wrote the article about which you wrote Mother Connelly. I have her address for you and was going to mail it to you."

He fumbled in his pockets until he found and gave to me the slip containing her full name and address: Mrs. Annie Sweeney, Ballybough Road. I visited her and Brother Furlong later.

Then we discussed my quest for Relics of Matt Talbot for the National Headquarters of The Matt Talbot Legion.

"I had a great many things that belonged to Matt," said Sir Joseph, "but unfortunately, I gave almost all I had to the Archbishop when he commandeered all Matt's Relics during the diocesan Process. However, from your letter to Mother Connelly, I learned that one of your objectives in coming to Dublin was to get some Relics of Matt and therefore I have put aside for you all I have, except one little Relic I'm keeping for myself."

Sir Joseph then handed me a large, thick envelope in which were contained his treasures: some generous portions of Matt Talbot's clothing and of his cotton blanket. These were the first Relics for The Matt Talbot Legion to fall into my possession and I especially valued them because they were given by Matt's first biographer.

Then I asked Sir Joseph what became of Matt's books and of the notes in his own handwriting, and he replied, "All these were commandeered by the Archbishop during the Process and he either still has them or has sent them to Rome."

I was of course disappointed, but I was to learn later that, just as Sir Joseph had not given everything to the Archbishop but had retained some Relics for himself, so others had done the same.

In connection with Matt's notes in his own hand from his reading, Sir Joseph said, "As far as we know, he wrote only one letter in his life. That was written when he was ill, in December, 1924, a few months before he died, to the Maynooth Mission for China where it is framed and on display."

I saw the letter later. It reads as follows: "Matt Talbot has done no work for the past 18 months. I have been sick and given over by priest and doctor. I don't think I will work anymore. Here is one pound from me and ten shillings from my sister." (See photograph on the next page).

"What became of Matt's iron bed on which he placed his planks and wooden pillow?" I asked.

"That is in the possession of one of his relatives," he answered, "but I don't know which one."

"Regarding the various places in which Matt lived," I

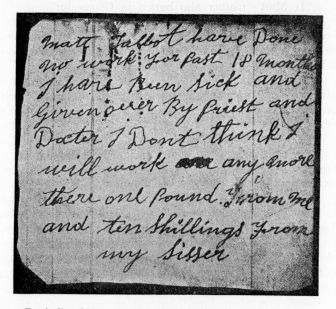

Facsimile of the only letter Matt Talbot is known to have
written.

asked, "I have three addresses: 13 Aldboro Court, where he
was born, and Gloucester Street (no number) where he
lived for a while, and 18 Upper Rutland Street, where he
spent all the latter years of his life. Will I be able to visit
all these places?"

"No," said Sir Joseph, "just 18 Upper Rutland Street.
We never could locate his room on Gloucester Street, and
his native place on Aldboro Court was destroyed by the one
bomb that fell on Dublin during the War. However it is
his room on Upper Rutland Street that is, in every sense,
his, and sanctified by his years of prayer and penance in it."

"I visited his grave in Glasnevin this noon, Sir Joseph.
The headstone is a beautiful one. Do you know its history?"

"Yes. When he was first buried, there was placed on
his grave only the very simplest marker, but my friend, Raphael O'Callaghan, influenced the priests and men of the
Sodality at St. Francis Xavier's to erect the present headstone. Raphael was one of the principal contributors."

"Is Matt's mother also buried in Glasnevin?"

"Yes, but it is not known where. She, like many of the very poor, was buried in an unmarked grave. It was known to Matt and his sisters who visited it, but now its location is unknown."

"That's a pity," I said, "for I had planned to visit the grave of his holy mother. Isn't it strange that after his death no one thought to ask his sisters the location of his mother's grave?"

"Yes," Sir Joseph answered, "but from another viewpoint not so strange, because Matt himself led a hidden life which would never have become known, had he not died wearing his chains."

"Speaking of chains," he continued, "you'd be interested to know that I met some years ago a lady, now dead, who knew Matt Talbot. She had asked him to join her in praying for a conversion. Matt agreed, and meeting the lady outside the church some days later, he said to her 'Nothing but the chains will do for that conversion,' and he persuaded her to let him get some chains for her. The conversion was obtained, and when I met her, she showed me the chain she was still wearing. She pulled a piece of the chain from underneath the neck of her dress."

We then discussed the question of why a man as strong-willed as Matt ever drank to excess in the first place.

"I have a theory," I said, "which is merely a guess. See what you think of it. I believe that it was a question of his instinct for sociability. There was no fun in his home, so many children living in cramped quarters, and the tavern was a much more pleasant place, where there was companionship of a kind. There were no movies and few distractions in his youth, and for those reasons, I think he just gravitated to the tavern."

"I think you're right," said Sir Joseph, "although it is also true that his older brothers drank to excess and he might have got the habit from them."

I then explained to Sir Joseph the purpose of The Matt Talbot Legion, and our hopes to help thousands of alcoholics through prayer and education. He was extremely enthusiastic as I unfolded our plans in detail. Since I knew from Mother Connelly that Sir Joseph was a very pious man, attending Mass every morning in spite of his blindness, I asked him to include the Legion in his prayers and requested also a message from him to the members of the Legion.

He replied, "I think it is a tremendous thing to get at alcoholics and an extremely Catholic plan of action to help them. I want to join the Legion. As for a message, tell them that I will pray daily with them and for them and for alcoholics and for the immediate and permanent success of The Matt Talbot Legion.

"I should tell you," he continued, "that one of Matt Talbot's first 'cures' was that of an alcoholic. It was a man who was brought to one of our city hospitals. While there he cried out one day, 'For God's sake, won't some one help me?'

" 'I will,' said a friend of mine, a nurse, and she had him kneel and recite with her the Prayer for Matt's Canonization. During the prayer, his voice gradually grew less strident and at its close, he rose and said quietly 'I'm cured.' The nurse paid little heed to the promise, but the man never drank again. I haven't heard of him in recent years but the last time I inquired, eleven years after, he was still a total abstainer."

"What does Rome think of the possibility of Matt's early canonization?" I asked. "Have you any news on that?"

"The Cardinal in charge is very enthusiastic," he answered. "He was much impressed by Matt's life and is anxious to expedite his Cause. He feels, as do many priests here, that in view of the spread of Communism in many countries, Matt's life is a timely example of what the Catholic faith can do to ennoble the life of laboring men."

It may seem strange to many readers that Sir Joseph Glynn, a wealthy man, should have in the first place been interested enough to write the life of a laborer. But all his life Sir Joseph has been the friend of the poor, and for many years has been an active official in that organization designed to help the poor and the afflicted, the St. Vincent de Paul Society of Dublin.

I next inquired, "How widespread is devotion to Matt Talbot in Ireland?"

He answered, "You can guess the general interest from

*Top left.* Father Ronald and Father Dolan in Matt Talbot's room. See Chapter 14. *Top right.* Exterior of the tenement at No. 18 Rutland Street, where Matt Talbot lived. His room is at the upper left. *Left.* Sir Joseph Glynn.

the sale of his life—350,000 copies to date. The war slowed down the devotion a little, but now the introduction of his Cause in Rome has given it new impetus here. As for other countries, the devotion to him is especially strong in Australia and Holland, and I have hopes that your Matt Talbot Legion will bring America to the fore in a short time.

"I turned on the radio the other night," he said, "and

was astounded to hear a voice speaking in English from a station in Holland saying, 'My subject tonight will be Matt Talbot.' "

Sir Joseph was naturally pleased when I told him that I had made the first American broadcast on Matt's life over the Columbia network in May of 1947.

Finally our talk turned to a discussion of the various pictures of Matt Talbot. Since no photograph of him exists, the various artists have been forced to paint him from word descriptions given by those who knew him. There is a wide difference between the paintings of him by Sean Dixon, by Sean O'Sullivan, by Sister Cecilia, and by Mother Nealis. According to Sir Joseph Glynn, the painting of Matt by Mother Nealis (see page 21) is the best and most accurate, although, as will appear later in these pages, his opinions in this matter have been challenged.

Sir Joseph said, "Mother Nealis has given us the best likeness of Matt. She forwarded her painting to me in an unfinished condition and I showed it to several who knew Matt. They were all impressed by its likeness to Matt and made some few criticisms and suggestions which I forwarded to Mother Nealis and which she incorporated in the finished picture."

In the course of my stay in Dublin, Sir Joseph and I talked over the telephone several times and I visited him briefly before leaving Dublin, but it was this first interview that was most important.

In leaving him that first day, I said, "Sir Joseph, I am eternally grateful to you for all the addresses and information you have given me and especially for the precious Relics."

"What I have given," he said, "I have given gladly and your visit gives me heart and hope for the future of Matt Talbot's Cause, especially in America. Your St. Therese will forward your work and I pray that our Matt will be ever at your elbow."

Aside from his invaluable assistance, I shall always remember, as one of the happy experiences of a life-time, this lengthy visit with this gentle, charming, Catholic gentleman, Sir Joseph Glynn. Sir Joseph's picture is shown on the facing page.

# 4.

## *Visit with the Archbishop of Dublin*

ON Monday, our second day in Dublin, Father Ronald and I made our way to the residence of the Most Reverend John McQuaid, Archbishop of Dublin. I presented to the Archbishop's secretary Cardinal Spellman's letter of introduction, in which His Eminence explained that I had written the first American life of Matt Talbot and was in quest of further and first-hand information concerning Matt in the interests of The Matt Talbot Legion.

We were not kept waiting long, but were soon ushered into the study of the Archbishop, who is gentle, soft-spoken and unhurried. His Grace received us with great courtesy, and listened attentively while I explained the purpose of our journey to Dublin in behalf of The Matt Talbot Legion.

"The Legion, Your Grace," I said, "is a movement of prayer and education to help alcoholics. It differs from a Total Abstinence Union in that it consists not merely of those who take a pledge but of all who want to help alcoholics. We hope to be of assistance to thousands of souls. For obvious reasons, we have taken Matt Talbot as our patron and therefore our Father Provincial sent us here to gain first-hand information about him from those who knew him and to secure perhaps one of his books and other Relics to place in the offices of the National Headquarters of the Legion."

The Archbishop said, "Your Father Provincial was very wise to send you. Otherwise, it would be asked, 'What, more than any other man, do you know of Matt Talbot?' Having visited all Matt's haunts in Dublin and his room and his surviving relatives and acquaintances, your experiences will give your Legion *authority*.

*Upper left.* Sean Dixon's picture of Matt Talbot. *Upper right.* Sister Cecilia's picture. *Lower left.* Mother Nealis' picture. *Lower right.* Sean O'Sullivan's picture.

"Unfortunately," he continued, "I can't help you too much in your quest of his books and Relics. My predecessor, Archbishop Byrne, commandeered all his known Relics and his books, and they were sent under seal to Rome when his Cause was introduced there. Everything was sent except his bed which the family refused to give up. However, I have an important Relic which I am prepared gladly to give to your Legion. It is a notable portion of the wooden pillow which Matt Talbot used."

To our delight, the Archbishop then produced the Relic, sealed with his red archiepiscopal seal and documented as follows: "Nos, Joannes Carolus, Archiepiscopus Dublinensis, Hiberniae Primas, testificamur hoc lignum esse particulam ex pulvino Venerabilis Servi Dei Matthaei Talbot. In quorum fidem praesentes litteras manu Nostra signatas sigilloque Nostro munitas fieri et expediri mandavimus. Datum Dublini die 18 mensis Augusti anni 1947."

Translated freely the document reads in English: "I, John Charles, Archbishop of Dublin, Primate of Ireland, testify that this wood is a portion of the pillow of the Venerable Servant of God, Matt Talbot. In testimony of this I have executed this letter signed with my signature and sealed with my seal. Given at Dublin, August 18, 1947."

If we were to secure nothing else, this notable Relic, so intimately associated with Matt Talbot's penitential life, assured the success of our journey. I tried to thank His Grace adequately.

"It is not probable but possible," said the Archbishop, "that you may find other Relics in the possession of some of his relatives, but if they have any, they will probably not wish to part with them, just as his relatives would not give up his bed. Father O'Donnell, the Vice-Postulator of his Cause, may be of help to you, and I suggest that you see him."

"Are you satisfied, your Grace," I asked, "with the present status of Matt's Cause in Rome?"

"Yes, and no. Yes, because everything possible is being done there to expedite things, and his life made a deep impression in Rome. No, because although we receive hundreds of reports of favors received through Matt's intercession, it is miracles we need. Conversions, cures of a non-miraculous nature, returns to the sacraments, employment secured, reform of drunkards—these we have in abundance; but these are hardly first-class miracles. It is miracles we need and you must have your Legion pray that Matt will produce them."

In reference to the Archbishop's allusion to the deep impression made in Rome by Matt's life, my readers will be interested in the following excerpt from the official organ of the Vatican, *Osservatore Romano*: "The Island of Saints, Missionary Ireland, offers today to Europe and to the world, the light of a new saintly son. We are confronted with a second Benedict Labre. The humble Irish workman, Matthew Talbot, has become a part of the history of the Church."

I then asked the Archbishop for a message to the members of The Matt Talbot Legion.

He said, "You are undertaking a noble and vitally important work in praying for alcoholics and in attempting to help all, especially the young, to understand in time the dangers of excess in drink. I shall pray for the members of the Legion and for its success. It is a shame that so far the care of alcoholics has been left to non-sectarian organizations. The Legion therefore fills a need. And this above all, make part of my message to the Legion: in your organization to help alcoholics, let prayer to Our Blessed Mother be dominant, for she is so maternal and protecting."

I explained to His Grace that The Matt Talbot Legion had two principal patrons, Our Blessed Lady and St. Therese, and that both Mary and Therese were part of the Legion emblem.

"With two such patrons, your Legion, named after the Venerable Matt Talbot, cannot but achieve its object," the Archbishop declared.

His Grace prolonged the conversation which covered many topics but I omit what does not bear directly on Matt Talbot. After consenting to be photographed with us (see page 12), our audience came to an end.

# 5.

## *Visit with the Vice-Postulator of the Cause, Father O'Donnell*

OUR next visit was to the pastor of the Church of the Immaculate Heart of Mary on City Quay. The pastor, Father Thomas O'Donnell, is the Vice-Postulator of the Cause of Matt Talbot. I had not been talking with Father O'Donnell ten minutes when I discovered that he and I had been fellow students in Rome years before. We had not then known each other, for he belonged to the Irish College and I to the American College, but we had been together in the same lecture hall at the Propaganda College in Rome, listening to lectures by professors, whom we recalled there in his Dublin study.

Father O'Donnell is a big, hearty man with a deep, vibrant voice and friendly manner. He needed no prodding to speak of Matt Talbot, to whom he is deeply devoted. In fact, although I am sure he would not want me to say so, I learned from Sir Joseph Glynn that Father O'Donnell, more than anyone else, influenced Archbishop Byrne to undertake the inquiry into Matt Talbot's Cause.

"I can never quite get over the manifest hand of Providence in Matt Talbot's case," declared Father O'Donnell. "Here was a workman who completely concealed his holiness and then Providence decreed that he should die on a public street and be brought to a public morgue and there his chains discovered and thus his hidden holiness revealed to all. There was the hand of God, there's no denying that," and his deep voice rumbled through the room with such power and conviction that I thought to myself, "I'd like to hear this man preach."

I told him something of my visit with Sir Joseph Glynn.

"There is one defect and one defect only in Sir Joseph's book," he said, "and that is that he does not bring out with

24

sufficient clearness that Matt was wholeheartedly on the side of the strikers."

"Matt wouldn't picket, would he?" I asked.

"No, but that doesn't prove that he wasn't in sympathy with the strikers. He struck when they did. As for picketing, you'd no more expect to find a man like Matt on a picket line than you'd expect to find him at a Bazaar. His fellow strikers understood that, and voted unanimously to give Matt strike pay even though he didn't picket.

"I knew Raphael O'Callaghan before he died," Father continued. "He was the man who lent Matt books. Raphael was a good man but the least bit snobbish. He was an employer. During the strike, the labor troubles were talked over between Matt and Raphael and they had hot words. Raphael testified to this during the diocesan Process. He was the only witness at the Process who called him 'Talbot;' the others called him 'Matt' or 'Mr. Talbot.' "

Right or wrong in his estimate of Raphael O'Callaghan, Father O'Donnell was arrestingly interesting and I could have listened to him indefinitely.

I told Father about our Matt Talbot Legion and about our quest of Relics, books and other things that belonged to Matt Talbot.

"I'm afraid you won't find too much," he said. "Everything that we could find was sent under seal to Rome except his bed with which the family would not part. I kept a few things for myself. I'll show them to you."

He unlocked a drawer in his desk and showed Father Ronald and me three links of Matt's chains, one of Matt's prayerbooks and a framed prayer to Jesus Crucified, which had been on the wall in Matt's room and which Matt recited daily.

I looked longingly at these precious treasures. I said, "You know, Father, if we had just one of those Relics in the United States, it would serve to bring Matt very close to the people who would see it, just as articles belonging to St. Therese make her seem very close to the people who visit our Little Flower Shrines."

"Yes," he said, " I know." Then skipping the whole question, he said, "I have his crucifix too. I'll show you that later. It is elsewhere on the premises."

I asked if Father Ronald could copy Matt's prayer to Jesus Crucified, which he permitted. It follows:

## Prayer to Jesus Crucified.

I adore Thee, O most sweet Saviour, Jesus, expiring on the cross for our sake. I have not words to express to Thee my gratitude for the infinite goodness Thou has evinced in dying to redeem me. O Eternal Father: I offer Thee Thy dear Son who hung on the tree of the Cross, naked, torn, pierced with thorns and nails, bleeding, anguishing, suffering, expiring. Yes, my God, it is Thy own and only begotten Son I offer to Thee in this lamentable condition; receive His divine sacrifice, accept this offering that I make Thee, it is my ransom, it is the Blood of a God; it is God Himself that I offer Thee now, for the payment and acquittal of my debts. I offer Him also for the relief of the Souls in Purgatory, of the sick, the poor and the afflicted, the grace of a happy death for the agonizing, the conversion of sinners, the perseverance of the just, and to impetrate for myself and for those specially dear to me the grace of dying in Thy Friendship and love, also the grant of their present urgent petitions. Amen. May the most holy and adorable will of God be ever accomplished in all things, may it be praised for ever and ever. *Amen.*

Father O'Donnell said, "If you'll come now, I'll show you Matt's Crucifix."

He conducted us downstairs and across the street from the rectory to his Catholic Social Service Kitchen. He explained that this was one of many Catholic Social Centres established by Archbishop McQuaid. In these centres, the poor of Dublin are fed and clothed. Five million meals were served in the centres last year. The Sisters of Mercy are in charge. If the poor are able-bodied, they come with containers and take away the warm meals. Pregnant women are served in the Centre by the Sisters. "They'll come to the Sisters," said Father O'Donnell, "for the Sisters ask no questions."

He conducted us to the main room of the Centre. There prominently displayed on the wall was Matt Talbot's immense Crucifix, formerly in Matt's room. On one side of it

*Above.* Pages from prayer book given by Father O'Donnell, Vice-Postulator of the Cause. *Left.* Father O'Donnell's letter of authentication.

was the picture of St. Therese! On the other, the picture of the Infant Jesus. There she was again, Saint Therese of the Child Jesus. It was as if she determined not to be left out of this Matt Talbot journey. Indeed Matt and Therese are linked inseparably in the Legion.

Father took the Crucifix from the wall and permitted us to be photographed with it. After we had inspected the immaculately clean Centre kitchens, of which Father was justifiably proud, we bade him farewell.

"I'll be back, Father," I said, "later in the week, for I'm hoping that you'll consider giving to The Matt Talbot Legion in America at least something from your rich store of Relics of him."

"Say a prayer that you can persuade me," he said. "It'll have to be a powerful prayer. But I'll be glad to see you again and hear your report on what you accomplish elsewhere. Come and take tea with me Thursday afternoon. Good luck to you."

I returned Thursday, but not precisely to take tea. I had in mind other things to take. Father O'Donnell wanted to know all the details of my visits since Monday. I told him about everything except the Relics I had received. That news I concealed and he'll read about it here for the first time. He laughed uproariously when I told him of my visit with the old lady who claimed to have given Matt his last drink. "You've seen more people in two days," he declared, "than I saw as Vice-Postulator. I marvel at it all. I think I'll hand over my job to you."

He roared again when I told him that I had been unable, to date, to find the "pub" or tavern which Matt patronized. "It should bear a sign," he said, "so that people could find it, a sign reading 'This is the pub where Matt Talbot had his last drink.'"

"Speaking of drink," he said, "I should have called your attention the other day to this. Come to the window here. There's the Customs House across the river. It was there that Matt worked with his father, and there he learned to drink whiskey. The bonded stores of liquor were kept there in Matt's time at the side and rear of the Customs House."

While we were having tea, he said, "I know what's on your mind. You'd like a link of Matt's chain. And if I can

28

get the Archbishop's permission, I'll give you a link. But I'll have to send it to you after you return."

I thanked him and then said, "I've been thinking of that prayerbook of Matt's that you have, Father. There is one section in it devoted to prayers to the Holy Face, the Little Flower's favorite devotion. Couldn't you cut out that section without spoiling the prayerbook and give it to me for the Legion?"

"I can," he said, "and I will." He reached for his keys and opened the treasure-drawer of his desk and extracted the prayerbook. Just then he was called away by the housekeeper to the parlor. He departed, leaving me before the open drawer. Returning in five minutes or so, he said, slyly, "Maybe I ought to count these treasures. Were you tempted to lift anything while I was gone?"

"I was tempted," I laughed, "but I conquered the temptation. I decided there'd be no blessing on Relics 'lifted', as you put it."

He then extracted the pages I had desired and gave them to me, and to say that I was overjoyed is an understatement. He wrote on his official paper as Vice-Postulator the document attesting the authenticity of the Relic. The document follows:

Office of the Vice-Postulator
of the Cause of the Beatification
and Canonization of the Servant
of God, Matt Talbot, Layman

I have given to Father Albert H. Dolan, O. Carm., these eight pages from a prayerbook which was the property of the Servant of God, Matt Talbot. The eight leaves are devoted to "Devotion to the Sacred Face of Our Lord, Jesus Christ."
(Signed) *T. O'Donnell,*
Vice-Postulator of the Cause
of Matt Talbot.

Then we reverted in our conversation to Matt Talbot. I asked him what I could do in America to expedite Matt's Cause in Rome. Would petitions for his canonization, bearing signatures, be of help? He said they would, and I am now

Father O'Donnell
with Father Ronald
holding Matt Talbot's
crucifix.

collecting, to forward to Rome, the signatures of Americans sincerely devoted to Matt Talbot and desirous of petitioning the Holy See for his early canonization. Such petitions in book form, are to be found at all our Carmelite Shrines of St. Therese.

I asked Father O'Donnell about the paintings of Matt Talbot. "Some—for instance Archbishop McQuaid—maintain that the best likeness is that painted by the Carmelite nun at Firhouse. Others—for instance Sir Joseph Glynn— say that Mother Nealis has painted the best likeness. Which opinion do you hold?"

"The majority of those who knew Matt Talbot, with whom I have talked," he said, "prefer the Carmelite nun's picture."

"Where is that convent?" I asked, "and what is the Sister's name who painted it?"

"I don't know her name but I can direct you to the convent. When do you want to go?"

"Now, this afternoon."

"Very well, We'll call a taxi and I'll give the directions to your driver."

We went to the street together and he was kind enough to call a taxi and give the directions. Father O'Donnell and I had two more visits later, but that was all that memorable Thursday afternoon. I departed with the treasured pages from Matt Talbot's prayerbook, reading them over and over again as the taxi rolled out of the city to the Carmelite Convent at Firhouse, a visit which is described later.

30

# 6.

## Visits with Matt's Fellow Laborers;
## Mr. Carew

READERS of my life of Matt Talbot know that the firm for which he worked for the last thirty-three years of his life was the T. and C. Martin Lumber Company. Because we had been told that some of Matt's fellow laborers still worked at Martin's, one of our first tasks in Dublin was to inquire who was now head of the firm. We learned that it was Mr. Thomas Martin. Martin, the family name of St. Therese of Lisieux!

We went to the main downtown office of T. and C. Martin and asked to speak with Mr. Thomas Martin. I had planned merely to obtain from him a list of his present employees who knew Matt Talbot. I explained to his secretary who I was and what I wanted. Mr. Martin immediately sent out word that he was ready to receive me. It seems the day before his wife had received a letter from her sister in England telling her that she was mailing to her an American life of Matt Talbot, *Matt Talbot, Alcoholic,* by a Father Dolan!

Mr. Martin proved to be a grand Catholic gentleman whose hospitality was perfect and help invaluable. He dropped everything and talked of Matt Talbot in answer to my questions.

"Yes, I knew him," he said. "In Matt's time my father was head of the firm and I had no direct dealings with Matt, but I often saw him in the Yard.

"I knew him from 1912 until 1925, the year of his death. I did not know him well. I never suspected his holiness, I just recognized him as one of our most reliable workers, steady and quiet and keeping to himself for the most part."

"Have you seen the various paintings of Matt Talbot?" I asked.

"Yes," he replied, "I've seen them all and I don't regard any of them as a very close likeness of him. The artists all give him an over-pious, sanctimonious expression. He wasn't like that. He always had a pleasant expression, almost jovial, almost as if he were about to smile. Moreover many of those paintings give him too much stature; he was a small man; shorter than the average and slight of build."

Mr. Martin was the first one we had visited in Dublin who had actually seen Matt and his description certainly brought Matt to life for us.

"Are there others here who knew Matt?" I asked.

"Yes, there are some here in these offices and some others in the Yard. Those in the Yard knew him best, but I'll call first those who are here."

In turn, the following, all former co-laborers with Matt and now all members of the firm, were summoned to tell us what they knew of Matt Talbot: Mr. John Byrne, now Secretary of the firm; Mr. Charles O'Kelly, Mr. William Powell and Mr. Joseph Stephens. In response to my questions, they divulged that they worked in the Yard with or near Matt Talbot from 1917 or 1919 to 1925. They said the same thing of Matt's appearance as Mr. Thomas Martin, all stressing Matt's pleasant expression. As they talked, these descriptive phrases recurred: "Always very quiet," "reliable" "not the usual run of workman," "not rough in speech but dignified." Not one of them even dreamed of Matt's holiness which he successfully concealed from all.

After these four members of the firm had been interviewed, Mr. Martin sent for a panoramic photograph of a large group of workmen in the Yard, taken in 1940. He pointed out to us a great many who had worked with Matt who had died since the photo was taken, and three others who are still living: Carew, Daly and Fuller.

"Could I interview these three men?" I asked.

"Certainly; they are in the Yard and we'll have to go to the Quay to see them. If you'll wait a minute until I dictate one letter I'll drive you myself."

"I have a taxi at the door. I kept it waiting because I thought I'd be with you only a few minutes."

Matt's favorite churches. *Above left*. Father Dolan kneels before the shrine of St. Therese in the Carmelite church in Clarendon Street. Matt Talbot made the first contribution to the erection of this shrine. *Above right*. The Franciscan church in Merchant's Quay. *Below left*. The Pro-Cathedral where Matt was baptized. *Below right*. St. Lawrence O'Toole's Church visited daily by Matt.

"I'll dismiss the taxi because you could never find these men alone. I'll go with you."

After his dictation, he conducted us to another office, unlocked a heavy safe and extracted a copy of a petition for Matt Talbot's canonization sent to the Holy Father in 1943, and signed by Mr. Martin and by other workmen who knew Matt Talbot. In the petition they gave testimony to the blameless, edifying life of Matt Talbot.

Then we set out in Martin's car for the lumber yard, on the Liffey, a ride of about thirty minutes along the river front.

We stopped first at Castle Forbes, which, in Matt's time, was the smaller of the two sections of the Martin Lumber Yards. Castle Forbes is so named from a castle formerly erected on that site by the Forbes family. In 1926, Castle Forbes was sold by the Martins who, at the same time, enlarged their properties in the other section. Now their holdings are much more extensive than in Matt's time.

It was in Castle Forbes that Matt worked from 1917 to 1925. It was here that there stood the small shed that was called Matt's "Office." In this shed, there was a telephone, installed during World War I; in this shed too Matt used to retire, whenever opportunity offered, to pray.

As we entered the Yard called Castle Forbes, I asked Mr. Martin what had become of Matt's "Office."

"I don't know," he said; "it was probably destroyed when alterations were made here after we sold the Castle Forbes section in 1926. But I'll inquire."

He took the time to make extensive inquiries, but no one knew what had become of Matt's "Office."

Mr. Martin then took us to the Martin Yard proper, where their properties along the river front are impressively extensive. It was in this section that Matt had worked from 1892 to 1917. Since he had been in Castle Forbes from 1917 to 1925, the total number of years of his employment by the Martin Company was thirty-three.

I walked through the Yard, peering into this shed and that corner, while Mr. Martin was occupied in rounding up, from various parts of the Yard, the three men, still working there, who had been co-laborers of Matt Talbot's.

The first to arrive was Mr. Daniel Daly, now fifty-three, and therefore thirty-one when Matt died. He remembered Matt well but had never been intimate with him.

"He was a very quiet man," declared Daly, "and made close friends of few, although we all liked him. Being so so much younger than Matt, I didn't get to know him well. Ed Carew, who is still here, knew him better than I. The only personal thing I remember about Matt is that one day when I had completely lost my temper and was raising ructions, Matt waited until I had calmed down and then said to me quietly, 'Dan, if you'd say a little prayer, you wouldn't lose your temper. Try it, me boy'."

Then Mr. James Fuller appeared. He is sixty-nine now, forty-seven when Matt died.

"I worked with Matt here," said Fuller, "from 1900 until he died in 1925. No, I never thought then that we would be looking forward now to the day when we'd be callin' him a saint. I did know him for a very religious man. He was a man who never bought a daily paper, but I've known him to think nothing of giving up to two pounds for a religious book or the life of a saint. If anyone took Our Lord's name in vain in his hearing, Matt would raise his hat. The men didn't like that at first, but after a while, a man would be ashamed to swear in Matt's presence. Not one of us older men would think of swearin' in his presence, any more'n we'd swear in front of the priest himself."

Then Mr. Martin returned, leading by the arm Mr. Edward Carew, who had been both Matt's fellow-worker and, for a time, his foreman. He is seventy-six now, fifty-four when Matt died. Mr. Carew was a gentle, charming old man, to whom I immediately took a special liking. He had known Matt better than the other two workmen, and therefore I decided to have a separate interview with him, which was arranged, and which I'll describe later.

The three men visited with us while Mr. Martin transacted some business in the main office. They asked many questions about devotion to Matt in America. They asked our opinion about how soon "the Holy See would be declarin' Matt a saint of God." They readily consented when I asked permission to return the next day with a photographer to take their pictures. (See the photos on Pages 44 and 84.)

Mr. Carew seized upon the first opportunity to take me aside. He asked if he could speak to me privately, and lead me behind the shelter of a lumber pile. There he reached into his inner coat pocket and drew forth an object covered by a linen handkerchief.

"This," he said, almost in a whisper, "is Matt Talbot's ruler!"

He let me examine it. Then he told me how it came into his possession.

"Matt used this ruler every day of his life," Carew said. "Every Saturday he would ask me to lock it up for him until a Monday. On Saturday, June 6, 1925, he gave it to me and said, 'Ed, will you lock up my ruler for me until Monday?' 'I will,' I said. He did not live till Monday, but fell dead that next day. That's how I come to have this ruler, which I've treasured now these twenty-two years."

I wanted to ask Mr. Carew a certain question then and there, but decided to wait. Instead, I said, "I can hardly imagine a Relic of Matt more precious and intimate than this working tool of his, unless it would be one of his prayer-books. How very fortunate you are."

"Yes," he agreed, "sometimes I think it is to this and to Matt that I owe many of my blessings."

I fingered the ruler long and covetously until, fearing I would keep Mr. Martin waiting too long, I handed it back to Mr. Carew, who wrapped it carefully and repocketed it as we rejoined Mr. Martin and the other two workmen.

Mr. Martin said to me in an aside, "I'll wager he showed you Matt's ruler. He is never without it"

I then asked all of them, Carew, Daly and Fuller, what had become of Matt's "Office," formerly in the Castle Forbes section of the Yard. Not one of them knew.

Then I asked, "Sir Joseph Glynn told me that the lodge-keeper at Castle Forbes and his wife are still living, the Mannings. Does anyone know their address?"

Mr. Carew, addressing Mr. Martin, said, "That would be Dan Manning."

"Oh, Dan Manning", said Mr. Martin. "Yes. I know

where he lives. We retired him on pension and I can find his home."

We said "Good-bye until tomorrow" to the workmen, and set off in the Martin car to find the Mannings.

# First Visit with Mr. and Mrs. Manning

WE drove along a pleasant street not far from the Yard and not far from St. Lawrence O'Toole's Church, where Matt used to make his "visit" to the Blessed Sacrament every evening. Mr. Martin stopped his car twice before he finally found the Manning home, a small cottage on Church Road, Eastwall. Both Mr. and Mrs. Daniel Manning were at home, old people, and as charming a couple as you could ever want to meet. Dan is a short, thin, old gentleman, polite and soft-voiced. But Mrs. Manning! I never dreamed of being fortunate enough to meet her, the lady who had prepared Matt Talbot's noon meal for him every day for years upon years. Mrs. Manning, of whose children Matt was so fond. She has a lovely countenance, the face of a Madonna, and the grace, dignity and humility of another Mary. I asked her little during that first visit, because I wanted to sit down with her alone, as I did later, and so I'll keep her reminiscences of Matt for a separate Chapter. I asked about her children, two of whom are pictured in the painting of Matt by Mother Nealis (see photo, Page 21), and arranged to visit her and her children later. After a short visit, Mr. and Mrs. Manning accompanied us out to the Martin car. Just before getting into the car, I asked Mrs. Manning the old question "You wouldn't know, would you, what became of Matt's 'Office?' "

"I have it," she said.

"You have it! Where?"

"In my yard. In the rear of my house."

We all made our way back to her home. Mrs. Manning led the way, and I walked with her. She said, "It is providential, Father, that you came and asked about Matt's 'Office' in the presence of Mr. Martin. Because it is in bad

*Left.* Mrs. Manning with Fathers Ronald and Dolan. Matt's "office" is in the background. See Chapter 7. *Right.* Miss Kate Byrne visits with Father Dolan. See Chapter 12.

repair and I've often tried to get the boldness to ask him to strengthen it. But he'll do it for you."

She conducted us through the house into the back yard and there in the corner was Matt's "Office." It is just a shed and on the point of falling apart. After inspecting it from without and entering it, I said to Mr. Martin, "But isn't it a shame that so important a Relic as this is so neglected?"

"I'll have a man here tomorrow morning," he said, "to put it in shape and I'll give orders that it be kept that way."

"Thank you, Mr. Martin," exclaimed Mrs. Manning, and she then gave me a grateful glance.

We had ourselves photographed with Mrs. Manning with Matt's "Office" as a background. (See photograph on Page 39.)

I asked Mrs. Manning if I could have a small piece of the wood of the 'Office" where Matt had so often prayed. She readily consented and Mr. Manning, with his huge knife, cut off a piece of the inner wall, and then, directed by Mrs. Manning, a piece of the exact plank, in the flooring, on which she said Matt used to kneel. Armed with these Relics, we said not "Good-bye" but "Au Revoir" to the Mannings.

Mr. Martin returned us to our hotel and if there is a finer gentleman in Dublin than he, I didn't meet him. He was kind enough to invite us to lunch with him the following Saturday at his home, and of course we accepted. Until that Saturday noon I had not had one free moment in Dublin. It was to be an afternoon of complete and delightful relaxation. Mr. Martin called for us at our hotel and drove us to his home near the ocean. His wife too is utterly charming. After lunch, she and her husband conducted us through their beautiful gardens, out of which come flowers that win prizes at the Dublin Flower Show every year. Then a ride was suggested. I said, "That gives me a chance to keep a promise. I promised Father Ronald that if my work here permitted any break at all, I would take him to see 'The Meeting of the Waters.' Would that be possible?"

Accordingly we drove out of Dublin through Bray and Greystone, into the hills of Wicklow. We were soon out "on top of the world," and were greeted with marvelous views at every turn, as we sped that afternoon through the glorious

Vale of Clara, through the wild, magnificent Glenmalure Pass, one of the grandest in Ireland, to Glendalough, which means "the Glen of Two Lakes." There we visited St. Kevin's seven churches, and then drove through wild country with superb views of the heather-clad mountains until, descending, we came through the Vale of Ovoca, to reach the Meeting of the Waters. It is the actual meeting place of the Rivers Avonmore and Avonbeg, and the legendary resting place where Tom Moore sat as he wrote the world-famous poem:

"There is not in the wide world a valley so sweet
As the vale in whose bosom the bright waters meet;
Oh! the last rays of feeling and life must depart,
Ere the bloom of that valley shall fade from my heart.

"Sweet Vale of Ovoca! how calm could I rest
In thy bosom of shade, with the friends I love best,
Where the storms that we feel in this cold world
    should cease,
And our hearts, like thy waters, be mingled in peace!"

# 8.

## *Further Visits with Mr. Carew;*
## *The Ruler*

AS agreed, the next day I returned to Martin's Lumber Yard with a photographer, who took pictures in the Yard of Daly, Fuller and Carew. Afterwards Mr. Carew and I had a private interview.

I explained to him the purposes and scope of The Matt Talbot Legion in America. I told him of the Relics already given by the Archbishop, Father O'Donnell, Sir Joseph Glynn and Mrs. Manning. I described my hopes of assembling, in one museum-like room at the Legion Headquarters, all the Relics of Matt Talbot I could obtain.

"Your ruler," I said, "would do more to bring Matt Talbot alive to those who see it in America than any of the Relics I have obtained so far. In your pocket it accomplishes little. In America it would serve to increase devotion to Matt."

To my surprise he replied, "I shall be glad to give it to you and to your Legion. I'm glad you asked for it, because I have been afeared that I'd lose it or that some one would take it from me or that after my death no one would value it. I give it to you gladly."

Suiting the action to the word, he withdrew the ruler from his inner pocket and handed it to me, linen wrapping and all. Overjoyed, I told him that I would keep him in my daily Mass and that the members of The Matt Talbot Legion would also surely remember him as one of their greatest benefactors. I ask the reader to say a prayer occasionally for this grand gentleman, Mr. Edward Carew. (See photograph of the ruler on page 44.)

I have said that I liked him from the moment I met him. Accordingly I invited him to call on me at our hotel that night. He appeared at seven and spent the entire evening with me. We talked of course almost exclusively of Matt Talbot.

One of his most revealing statements was this. "It may seem strange to you," he said, "but I never knew, until after Matt's death that he ever drank. When I heard, after his death, of his years of drunkenness, I could hardly believe it. It was so contrary to all that he was and all that I knew of him. Besides we often exchanged confidences about our youth and never a word did he speak to me about the drink. The worst he ever told me about himself was that as a mere boy he used to catch goldfinches by setting out decoys and bird-lime, so that when they sat on it, they couldn't get off. Never a word about the drink."

As Mr. Carew spoke, he shook his head doubtfully and regretfully, as if either he still couldn't believe that Matt ever drank, or that it was scarcely fair of Matt to keep it from him.

Prodded by my questions, he poured forth his memories of Matt. "I recall," he said, "that on one occasion a priest was taking a collection in the Yard for his poor church in a remote part of Ireland and Matt gave to him his entire week's wages.

"Matt wouldn't let us catch him at it, but we knew from Dan Manning who got it from his children, that, when we were taking the full lunch hour to eat and smoke and talk, Matt spent most of his lunch hour in his 'Office' at prayer.

"I guess I fell into his bad graces for a while one Ash Wednesday morning when before the lunch hour, I said to him, 'We can take milk in our tea today, I hear, because of the Archbishop's dispensation from the black fast on account of the epidemic.' From his expression, I think Matt was riled at me for availing myself of the dispensation when it was not meant for the likes of me. But he said nothing. I would wager that he had no milk in his tea that day."

"Did you or the workmen regard Matt," I asked, "as a kind of holier-than-thou type?"

"Not at all," he replied. "He forced his way of life on nobody. We all respected him. It was wonderful to see him handle some of the rougher men. Some of the truck drivers worked on piece work and were so paid, and if they had to

43

*Above.* Father Ronald and Father Dolan with three of Matt's fellow laborers in the Martin Lumberyard. Mr. Carew is in the center; at the left is Daniel Daly and at the right, James Fuller. *Below.* Matt Talbot's ruler. This ruler is now in the Matt Talbot Legion Museum in Englewood, N. J.

wait, some of those terrible, rough bullies would be in a temper, but when they went in to Matt, it was wonderful to see how he could handle them. They came out meek as lambs, whatever he said to them."

"Did you know anything about his wearing penitential chains?" I asked.

"I did not. I never dreamed of it. He was not a man to do anything for show.

"But I went into his 'Office' on an errand one day when he was in another part of the Yard and I saw cinders on one of the boards on the floor. The cinders couldn't get in there unless Matt put them there purposely. I guessed that he put them there to kneel on, in penance, when he prayed. But I never mentioned it to him, for I knew he wouldn't want me to know what I had discovered.

"One day, Matt told me that he was reading in the Bible the night before the Book of Deuteronomy. I said, 'Matt, do you understand it?' He answered 'Before I read it, I go on my knees and pray to the Holy Ghost for light to understand it, and I think I understand enough to do me some good.'

"Neither the weather nor anything else made any difference in his order of day. Nothing would keep him from his daily Mass. He used to say to me of a cold winter's morning, 'Brother Furlong was terribly late this morning in opening the church doors at Gardiner Street.'

"And tired as Matt was, or late as it might be, his first stop on leaving the Yard was at St. Lawrence O'Toole's Church."

Towards the close of our visit, Mr. Carew asked a favor of me. He has a sister in Forest Hills, Long Island. He had not heard from her in seven months. Would I communicate with her upon my return to America and inform him if all was well with her. I promised to do so, and upon my return, I looked her up immediately, and found her feeble but in good health considering her age, nearly eighty. That same day, I sent by air mail my report of his sister to Mr. Carew. That was the least I could do for this grand old gentleman and I trust it is not the last favor I can do him.

# 9

# Second Visit with the Mannings

AS I have previously related, I arranged, during my first visit with Mr. and Mrs. Manning, to visit them again later. As I understood the arrangement, I was to call at their home on Church Road and they would have their daughters there for the visit. Accordingly I arrived at their home at the time appointed, but discovered that only Dan was home, and that I was expected at their daughter's home, to which Mrs. Manning had already gone.

So I persuaded Dan to come with me in the taxi to the daughter's home in another part of Dublin. It was Dan's first ride in a taxi! He enjoyed it immensely and sat up straight, proud as a peacock. As we rode, we talked about Matt Talbot.

"It was my wife," he said, "who knew him best. I seldom came in contact with him, but I knew him, as everyone did for a very good, religious-minded man. My wife knew him very well, for she prepared his noon meal for him every day.

"I remember," he continued, "speaking to Matt at length only once. On that occasion, I was sent to his part of the Yard at a time when he was not occupied, and I found him sitting on a pile of lumber reading. I said, 'What is the book, Matt?' He showed it to me. It was Cardinal Newman's Apologia. I asked, 'Do you understand that, Matt?' and he replied, 'I do. Enough of it, in any case. Before I read I say a prayer to understand it. Otherwise I'd not get the sense of it.'"

"During his life time," I asked, "were you impressed with Matt?"

"I was," he replied. "Everyone was. All the men were— everyone of them that I knew. But none of us thought we would be talking of him one day as a saint."

Mr. Dan Manning

As we neared our destination, Dan asked, "When will they canonize him, Father? Will it take years or will it be soon? Wouldn't it be grand if we who knew him could live to see him called a Saint?"

Before recording my visit with Mrs. Manning, it will be well to insert here these paragraphs concerning her from my life of Matt Talbot.

"Matt took precautions lest any adult should see him at such prayers, but certain children saw him and told their mother. With this mother, Mrs. Manning, who was the wife of the lodgekeeper at Castle Forbes, Matt had at times brief conversations. She reports that he was always gentle and un-assuming, but that he would not discuss news and always brought the conversation round to the lives of the saints.

"The children were the daughters of the lodgekeeper who lived in a house at the Yard gate. The children liked Matt and Matt was fond of the children, especially of Teresa, to whom he would often speak of St. Teresa, telling her to pray to her for anything she wanted and she would get it. Whether he thought the children at their play would pay little attention to him kneeling at prayer in his "Office," or whether he believed that they would benefit by his example, the fact is that he did not mind their nearness while he prayed.

"Incidentally, Matt never forgot the children at Christmas time. On Christmas Eve when the Yard was closed, there was always the same ceremony. While the children waited anxiously, Matt searched his pockets pretending that it was difficult to find the gifts. Then he would produce a coin carefully rolled up in several bits of paper which he solemnly unrolled, one by one, until the coin was revealed, and given to each child. However, in the course of years, the number of children in the family increased until there were seven, so that Matt had to reduce the size of the coins, but he went through the same procedure with the seven silver pieces. He was no morose recluse, no eccentric hermit, but a lovable, warmly human person, ever cheerful, ever kindly, ever willing to help his fellows."

Arriving at his daughter's home, Dan and I mounted the steps to her flat and there found Mrs. Manning, two of her daughters, Mona and Catherine, and a house full of grandchildren. Mrs. Manning introduced me to Catherine and Mona, both now married. I asked them if I could speak to their mother first and then afterwards to them. Dan went to play with his grandchildren and I was left alone with Mrs. Manning.

She told me first of her family. She had nine children. Three are dead. Of the six still living, all girls, three are married, three unmarried. All, except the very young children, knew Matt Talbot. Catherine is now thirty-eight; sixteen when Matt died. Mona is thirty-four; twelve when Matt died. Teresa, who, with the other three younger daughters, was then on vacation in another part of Ireland, is thirty-two, ten when Matt died. The two Manning children who are pictured with Matt in Mother Nealis' painting (See Page 21), are Teresa and Mary, who is dead. Mary died at twenty-one and is buried near Matt in Glasnevin.

Mrs. Manning said, "I think he was fondest of Teresa, because she was the youngest at the time and because he had great devotion to St. Teresa. He had a lot to do with Teresa and she knew him best. She was very obliging to him. But he was very nice and friendly with all the children. At Christmas time he'd distribute to them very solemnly the presents he had for them, coins wrapped in paper. He'd unwind the paper slowly, as they looked on wonderingly and expectantly."

As we talked there in the Manning parlor of her daughter Teresa, I was conscious of the picture of the Little Flower, looking down from the wall at us as we talked. She was everywhere in Dublin.

*Upper left.* Mrs. Lydon and Father Dolan. See page 56. *Upper right.* Father Dolan with Martha Doyle and Brother Nolan. See Chapter 11. *Lower left.* Officer Hanlon with Father Dolan. See page 63. *Lower right.* Father Ronald with Dr. Eustace. See page 56.

I said, "Mrs. Manning, I think I know most about your contacts with Matt but I'd like to hear it from your own lips."

"Well," she said, "I saw him every day except Sunday. He came to me every day at noon for his can. I made his noon meal for him daily."

"What did he eat at noon?"

"A scrap of cocoa and a scrap of tea mixed and made with boiling water and then allowed to get stone cold. That's all he'd ever take at noon."

"Did you know that he was doing it as a penance?"

"I did not. That is, I wasn't sure, because he never said so. But I guessed his reason. He was a sensible and very human man, as well as a holy one. I tested him once to see if his mind was really on his food at all. One day I was busy and wanted to get out of the kitchen and his water was not quite boiled. I said to myself 'That will do. He'll not notice the difference.' The next day he said to me, 'Would you make sure the water boils? That wasn't boiled yesterday.'"

I asked, "How did you ever imagine in 1926, less than a year after his death, that his 'Office' would ever be worth keeping? What gave you sufficient foresight to go to the foreman when Castle Forbes was being altered and arrange to have his 'Office' transferred from the Yard to the backyard of your home?"

She replied, "I always had a wish for Matt Talbot. I always knew that he was different from other men. He always struck me so.

"There's one thing he said," she continued, "that I'll always remember. I tell it often to my children and to my grandchildren. One day he was at my back door and I saw Mr. Martin coming and I said to him, 'You'd better be off, Mr. Talbot, Mr. Martin is coming.' He replied, 'Never be afraid of any man. One Person only is to be feared as well as loved: God.' I tell my children to take those words as their motto: 'Never be afraid of any man. One Person only is to be feared as well as loved: God.'"

We were speaking again of Matt's penances, so successfully concealed from all: his chains and his nightly vigils, when Mrs. Manning said "He was not a man for show. Once at Christmas time, he happened in just when we were eating our Christmas pudding. He took some, but I knew that it was because he wouldn't pretend to us that it was not his habit to take desserts. He wouldn't let on that he was used to doing penance."

After Mrs. Manning had completed her reminiscences of Matt, she called in Dan, and her daughters, Catherine and Mona. I questioned the daughters each in turn.

In response to my questions, Catherine said, "I remember him, but not very vividly. I can recall nothing much about him except handin' out his can of tea and cocoa to him every noon."

Mona said, "I too recall his coming to our back door for his can, but I remember best his Christmas presents. (All the Mannings laughed at this.) He'd have the coins in his inside pocket, but he'd first look in all his other pockets, pretending that he couldn't find our presents."

Mrs. Manning interjected, "He reduced the six penny pieces when the children began to multiply too fast for his purse."

The family accompanied me to the door downstairs, and before we said farewell, I was taken into the court to look at their youngest grandson, basking in the sun in his carriage. I wonder if he'll ever know what a saintly grandmother is his. I regard Mrs. Manning as in every way fitted to be, as she was, the intimate associate of the saintly Matt Talbot.

It was a marvelous experience to find ourselves in actual touch with relatives and friends and acquaintances of Matt Talbot. Furthermore it was wonderful to see reflected in them the holiness which had spread from Matt Talbot to those around him. How unconsciously they revealed their own beautiful lives, as they told us stories of their saintly friend. And how deeply, as I listened, did I realize that these were the true types of our Irish people and not the wretched degenerates the so-called National Theatre presents to the world as types of Catholic Ireland.

# 10.

## *Further Visits with Mrs. Purcell;*

## *Her Gifts*

I HAVE already described the beginning of my acquaintance with Mrs. Susan Purcell, who is in charge of "The Mission" shop in Granby Lane, a few steps from the spot where Matt Talbot died. She had made me the promise, which she kept, that, on account of our common devotion to St. Therese and to Matt Talbot, she would help me in Dublin in every way possible. I visited with her every day of my stay in Dublin.

She had been for years a fellow sodality member of Mrs. Mary Andrews, Matt Talbot's sister, who died in 1934 in Matt's own bed. Mrs. Andrews and Mrs. Purcell had been close friends and had discussed Matt times without number. Moreover it was Mrs. Andrews herself who had given to Mrs. Purcell her "treasures:" his books and specimens of Matt's own handwriting.

Next to Sir Joseph Glynn, Mrs. Purcell knew more about Matt Talbot than anyone I met in Dublin. It was second-hand information because she herself never met Matt, but her long years of friendship with Matt's sister were fruitful of the most exhaustive fund of knowledge about Matt. Moreover in her devotion to Matt, she had made it her business to seek out and talk with everyone who had had any connection, even the most remote, with Matt. She was untiring in her efforts to arrange interviews between all these people and me. It was she who aranged my interviews with all the people mentioned in this Chapter and Chapters 11 and 12 of this book.

"I feel that I am most fortunate," she said to me one day, "to be in charge here in Granby Lane, for it was here he died; it was here that he was given to the world."

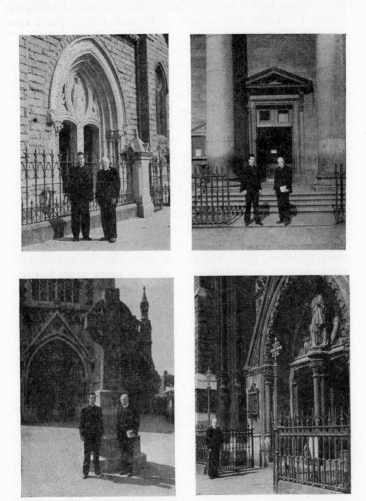

Matt Talbot's favorite churches. *Upper left.* Fathers Ronald and Dolan before Matt's parish church, St. Joseph's on Berkeley Road. *Upper right.* Before the Jesuit church, St. Francis Xavier's, on Gardiner Street. *Lower left.* Before the Vincentian Church in Phibsboro. *Lower right.* Before the Augustinian church in John's Lane.

On another occasion she confided to me, "If I lose anything I find myself saying 'Matt, find it for me.' I wouldn't bother the Little Flower with such small things, but I can speak to Matt about them. I feel that he's about; he's here."

We looked over together her register which contains the signatures of bishops, priests and lay people who had visited Granby Lane. I copied, as she read them to me, some addresses of far-off places noted in the register: Nigeria, Liberia, Australia, Chicago, San Francisco, Seattle, the Philippines, Saginaw, Saigon in China and of course there were hundreds of signatures from all parts of Ireland, and from Glasgow, London and Edinburgh.

When I called in Granby Lane in the evening, Mrs. Purcell was sure to call my attention to the "Thank you, Matt Talbot" items in the paid advertising section of the Dublin daily papers that particular day.

She had saved for years clippings of articles concerning Matt that had appeared in the daily papers and we read them together. There was one of particular interest; it told the story of a mysterious lady who for many years has appeared at Glasnevin Cemetery Gate every morning at precisely eight o'clock when the gates open. She comes rain, shine or snow, summer and winter. She walks through the cemetery to Matt's distant grave, kneels there for her prayers, and leaves, refusing to give her name to anyone.

"Who do you think she could be, Father?" asked Mrs. Purcell.

"I haven't the slightest idea," I replied.

"People say," she volunteered, "that it is the girl who offered marriage to Matt and he refused."

I laughed loudly at this amusing guess. "That's women's gossip for you," I said.

Mrs. Purcell didn't like that at all. "It could be, couldn't it?" she asked. "Who else would be so devoted to him?"

"Why, you yourself are just as devoted to him in a less spectacular way. You're here in the Lane every day, giving your time to him and to his Cause, and keeping fresh flowers at his little Shrine here. Maybe you're keeping things from us. Maybe you're the lady 'who offered marriage to Matt and he refused.'"

Mrs. Purcell with Father Dolan.

She looked at me reproachfully and the subject was dropped. But let me not create the impression that Mrs. Purcell was without a sense of humor. Speaking of people taking bits of clay from Matt's grave, she once said to me, "If everyone who visits his grave continues to take a bit of clay from it, they'll have him exhumed before his Beatification."

"Speaking of his Beatification," she continued, "there is a lady near here, a Mrs. Catherine Lydon, who was present in the Lane here when Matt fell dead. She says that Father Walsh, who was the priest called to Matt's side, predicted that one day Matt would be beatified and his remains exexhumed and carried into the Pro-Cathedral. Would you like to talk to Mrs. Lydon?"

Of course I agreed and Mrs. Purcell locked up "The Mission" and accompanied me to Mrs. Lydon's home. She is a very old lady (See photo, Page 49), and did not know Matt in life. Everything she told me is incorporated in this statement signed by her and now on display, framed, in The Matt Talbot Museum in Englewood, N. J. It follows:

August 20, 1947.

I, Catherine Lydon, 31 Upper Dorset, Dublin was present when Matt Talbot fell dead on the left hand side of the road leading from Parnell Square in Granby Lane on Sunday, June 7th, 1925, and I witnessed Father Reginald Walsh, O. P., and Dr. Eustace, Parnell Square, attend the deceased who, they said, had died at once. Father Walsh said to me, "I won't live to see the day, but you will live to see the remains of holy Matt being carried up the steps of the Pro-Cathedral, Marlborough Street."

God grant his words will come to pass!

(Signed)   Mrs. Catherine Lydon

Another day, Mrs. Purcell arranged that the Dr. Eustace, mentioned in Mrs. Lydon's statement, should meet us in Granby Lane, where he and Father Ronald were photographed together. (See Page 49.) Dr. Eustace, like Mrs. Lydon, had never seen Matt in life. He said, "He had crossed the Jordan before I arrived; his pulse had ceased."

It was Mrs. Purcell's idea that Dr. Eustace and Mrs. Lydon should give me signed statements. That of Dr. Eustace may also be seen now in The Matt Talbot Museum in Englewood. It reads:

August 21, 1947.

I, Doctor E. P. Eustace, attended Matt Talbot on June 7. 1925, when he died in Granby Lane on his way to the Dominican Priory Church. He died on the left side of the road about three feet from the path on the way from Parnell Square. He died, in my opinion, from heart failure.

(Signed)   Edward Patrick Eustace, M. D.<br>30 Parnell Square,<br>Dublin

In the course of our visits, Mrs. Purcell had me relate to her all that took place in Lisieux, from where I had just come, and all that transpired during my latest visit with the two living Carmelite sisters of St. Therese. She asked about Pierre who years before had given me his Little Flower crucifix for our National Shrine of St. Therese in Chicago. She was distressed to learn of his death. It would be difficult to say which was stronger in Mrs. Purcell, devotion to the Little Flower or to Matt Talbot.

Almost every time I visited Mrs. Purcell, I asked her to let me see and handle again her "treasures:" the things she possessed that had been the property of Matt Talbot. Finally, I summoned the courage to say to her, "Which of these are you going to give me for our Matt Talbot Legion in America?"

"I knew you were going to ask me for these," she said. "I know you; I know you from your book about your first visit to Lisieux. Years ago I read about the Relics of St. Therese you secured from Pierre and from the sisters of St. Therese. Oh, yes, I knew you were going to ask for my Relics of Matt."

But she said nothing further; there was silence for a while. Finally she said. "Say a prayer to your Therese in your Mass tomorrow that I'll have the grace to be generous with you."

The next morning, she handed me a large envelope, and a smaller one which contained this letter.

Dear Father Dolan,

I give you herewith the two papers in holy Matt's own handwriting. I got these from his sister, Mrs. Andrews, my dear friend.

These have been my most cherished possessions all these years, but knowing what you have done to make Little Therese (Matt's "brave little girl") known in America, sure I couldn't refuse, knowing what you will do for our own Matt in our Greater Ireland beyond the seas.

May God bless your work is the sincere prayer of

Yours respectfully,
(Signed)    *S. Purcell*

Two of Matt Talbot's prayer books and, in the center, a page from his *Life of Christ*. Matt's handwriting may be seen on the upper prayer book. These are now in the Matt Talbot Legion Museum in Englewood, N. J.

I said, "Mrs. Purcell, I have seldom received a more beautiful letter than this. I'll cherish it almost as much as your precious pages of Matt's own handwriting."

The pages she gave me are shown on pages 65 and 67. One page contains notes Matt made in the Lumber Yard. These notes consist of measurements of the lumber he handled as 'storeman.' The other page is a passage Matt copied in his own hand from a religious book he borrowed. The passage reads: "The pain of loss arises from the ceasing of the intercourse between the soul and its Creator. By the pain of sense is meant the torment of fire. The fire of hell is a corporeal fire."

This copied passage is a splendid proof that this self-educated laboring man, who left school at the age of twelve, understood perfectly what he read in the theological books he borrowed.

I had scarcely time to thank Mrs. Purcell for her magnificent gifts, when she produced Matt's copy of Fouard's life of Christ, published by Gill in Dublin in 1908. "It seems to me," she said, "that you could take some pages from the middle of this book without spoiling the book. Then we would both share the book together."

Accordingly we gently removed Pages 107 to 110, inclusive, from Matt's book and they are now to be seen in The Matt Talbot Legion Museum in Englewood.

I felt that, even though I would be risking Mrs. Purcell's displeasure, I must make some kind of offering to her in return for all these precious Relics she had given. So I put a generous offering in an envelope and as I was leaving I handed it to her, saying, "Here is something for you to open after I leave. Use it for the poor, or for Matt's Cause or for yourself. It is a feeble way of expressing my thanks." I walked out the door before she could reply.

The next day at the hotel I received a registered letter from Mrs. Purcell, in which she returned the offering I had given. Her letter read:

Dear Father Dolan,

You took me by surprise this afternoon in giving me the envelope. I sure appreciate your kind thought, but oh, my, I am returning it now, as I want to sleep tonight. I know you wished me to give it to some charity to honor Matt, but even so, it burns.

I was so happy to meet you and help you, but this offering would just spoil the joy I have had these few days, which I wish you could multiply. If at any time I can be of any assistance to you, even should you return another year, I am here at your service.

I am just thrilled through and through by what you are doing for my Matt and overjoyed to have had a small part in your work for him.

I forgot to give you the portions of Matt's woolen sock and cotton blanket given to me by his sister, Mrs. Andrews. I enclose them.

When we are in Rome together for Matt's canonization will we not say together "Deo Gratias?"

I remain, dear Father,

Yours respectfully,

(Signed)   S. Purcell

After reading the letter, I dropped everything I had planned, and hurried over to Granby Lane to see Mrs. Purcell. I said to her, "Without any exception, that letter of yours is the most beautiful, most heart-warming letter I have ever received. I'll cherish it always. I felt, and I know you felt, that we were friends; now we both *know* it. I am profoundly grateful to you, grateful beyond words, for all you have done, and done so generously, unselfishly, and with one single-minded purpose: to advance Matt's Cause. I want you to know that you can call on me and count on me anytime, anywhere for anything. But I simply must find some way of expressing my gratitude to you before I leave. Isn't there something I can do for you?"

"There is," she said tearfully, "if I could only have one of your Masses offered for me while you are here in Dublin. A Mass in honor of Matt and the Little Flower offered for me. And could I be bold enough to ask one more great favor? You can say 'No' and I won't be hurt. You told me of the little Relics the sisters of St. Therese gave you last week, the

Relics on holy cards that her sisters touched with their own hands. Could I have one of those?"

"You'll have the Mass tomorrow morning," I assured her, "and I'll bring the Relic of St. Therese to you before the day is over."

Mrs. Purcell's piety, courtesy and hospitality is typical of what, in my experience, is general throughout Ireland. Everywhere and from everyone, high and low, from the Archbishop, from the civic officials of Dublin, from Sir Joseph Glynn, from Mr. Thomas Martin, from the workmen, as from Mrs. Purcell, I received what I call 'perfect hospitality and perfect courtesy.' It would suit me fine if, to Ireland's proud title "The Isle of Saints and Scholars," these further words were to be added: "and of perfect courtesy and perfect hospitality."

Mrs. Purcell continued, as long as I remained in Dublin, to be as helpful as she had been before she gave to me her precious Relics. It was she who arranged my interviews with Mrs. Annie Sweeney, to whom one Chapter of this book is devoted. It was Mrs. Purcell too who persuaded the following to come to Granby Lane on successive days to meet me: Catherine Carrick, Officer Hanlon, Brother Nolan, Mary Roberts, John Daley, and Martha Doyle. We meet these people in the following Chapter.

# 11.

## *Visits with Other Relatives and Acquaintances*

### *John Daley*

JOHN DALEY now works at Jordan's Furniture Manufacturing Company in Granby Lane. He is fifty-six years of age. He is a very well-spoken workman, and enthusiastic about the rapid progress of Matt Talbot's Cause so far. He did not know Matt Talbot to speak to but knew him by sight. I submit in Daley's own words his statements concerning Matt.

"Matt, when I knew him first, was a little old man. I used to see him kneeling in St. Saviour's (Dominican) Church where I was an usher and a member of the sodality. Upon entering the church before the first Mass, when no one else was there, he would always follow the same routine: he would walk up to the top of the center aisle, genuflect to the Blessed Sacrament, kneel and kiss the pavement; then he would go to the Blessed Virgin's altar, kneel and kiss the steps of the altar; then, after his prayer there, he would retire to the back of the church and kneel in an inconspicuous place. When I saw him kissing the pavement, I said to myself, and I'll repeat my exact words, as perhaps I shouldn't, 'That man's a first-class idjut (idiot) or a first-class saint.'

"The morning Matt died here in Granby Lane, my pal, Sebastian Bregazzi, Prior of the Third Order Dominicans, went to get Father Walsh, O. P., for Matt. He could not find Father Walsh, and Father Gaffney, O. P., was about to go (he was nearly vested for Mass), when Father Walsh appeared and said 'You go on and say Mass; I'll go on the sick call.' Afterwards, Father Gaffney, when he learned who the man was who died in the Lane, was disappointed that he didn't go instead of Father Walsh. Father Gaffney is now at Black Abbey,

Kilkenny. Father Gaffney, at the Mass that morning was the first to ask prayers for Matt Talbot from the altar, although, not knowing his name, he asked for prayers 'for a man who had just died in Granby Lane.' "

## Officer Hanlon

Thomas Hanlon, a Dublin policeman, called "Officer Hanlon," is now forty-nine. (See page 49.) When Matt Talbott died, he was twenty-seven and had been only twelve months on the police force. Officer Hanlon's statement follows in his own words:

"I was on duty in Parnell Square and Granby Lane, June 7, 1925, a Sunday. A small boy came to the top of the Square and shouted to me, 'A man has just dropped dead in the Lane.' I arrived at the man's side just as the ambulance came. The priest had been there before I was called. I had to give a report of his death and so I went in the ambulance to the morgue. I found nothing in his pockets, except a prayerbook and rosary. I turned down his shirt, with the Sister, to look for a laundry mark and it was then we saw the chains. Late that evening I found his sister at Rutland Street and she identified him at the morgue the next morning."

## Miss Mary Roberts

Her statement throws a tiny ray of light on Matt's life or death. She says:

"On the morning Matt died, I was in Granby Lane. I saw six men near the end of the Lane, at the side of the church. They were men of the sodality to which Matt belonged. They had stopped on account of Matt, whose body was lying in the Lane. I went over and looked at him. I remember that he wore a striped workingman's shirt, gray trousers and clean boots. His eyes were turned up and glazed. I was there a few minutes before Doctor Eustace came. Shortly after the ambulance arrived and Matt's body was taken to the hospital."

Brother Nolan belongs to the Maynooth Mission to China. He happened to be in Granby Lane one day while I was there and Mrs. Purcell introduced me to him. He had come to say a prayer at the spot where Matt died. He said, "I was only thirteen when Matt died. I was at the church door that morning of June 7 when word came that a man had dropped dead on Granby Lane. It was out of mere curiosity that I ran to see him. I took him for an ordinary workman. Later when I read his life, I began to practise and still practise daily devotion to him."

## Mrs. Catherine Carrick

Mrs. Carrick, who before her marriage was Kitty Kelly, is now seventy-eight. She is a tiny, wizened old lady, frowzy and unkempt. My interview with her was extremely brief. Her parents owned the tavern which Matt frequented. In that tavern, she was in her youth a bar maid. As such, she claims, she gave Matt his last 'pint of porter', the day before he took his pledge. She remembers nothing of Matt except that, in his drinking days, he used to sweep and clean up the tavern to earn a few extra shillings. She never saw Matt after the day before he took his pledge.

## Miss Martha Doyle, Matt Talbot's Cousin

On one of the latter days of my stay in Dublin, I received this letter sent by special messenger to the hotel by Mrs. Purcell:

Dear Father Dolan,

I have asked Miss Martha Doyle to meet you here in Granby Lane this afternoon. She is Matt's first cousin. You usually come to Granby Lane about three; so I asked Miss Doyle to come at that time. You will be pleased, because she

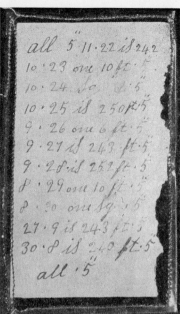

Specimens of Matt Talbot's handwriting. The figures are records he made in the lumber yard. These are now in the Matt Talbot Legion Museum in Englewood, N. J.

has something for you, which belonged to Matt. I hope you will be able to come. I remain, dear Father,

Yours respectfully,
S. Purcell

I was of course there at the appointed time to meet Martha Doyle, a smartly dressed, rosy-cheeked, middle-aged lady. (See photo, page 49.) She had with her a copy of the May 19, 1943 issue of a magazine in which there was an article written by her entitled "My Cousin, Matt Talbot."

In reply to my questions, Miss Doyle stated:

"My mother's maiden name was Mary Talbot. She was the sister of Matt Talbot's father.

"You will be interested to know that Matt's father and the Little Flower's father looked very much alike. One was the perfect image of the other.

"My mother often used to speak of Matt's charity and love of neighbor. She told me that if in Matt's presence something ill was said of a neighbor, Matt would palm it all off and smooth it over.

"Mrs. Fylan, Matt's sister, told me that she went over to see Matt the Saturday night before he died, and as she sat talking with him, she observed the brightness of his eyes and his high color. She remarked 'You look splendid'. He replied 'I never felt better in my life'. That's the last she saw of him in life.

"I was four years of age when my cousin, Matt Talbot, visited us. He was young then; he had just taken the pledge for life. He played with us, laughed with us, told us stories, my sister, my brothers and myself. His sister, Mrs. Susan Fylan, told me in later years, that I had been his favourite.

" 'I like the little fair girl, Martha,' he said to Susan one evening, when she asked him which of the children he liked best. I was grown up when Susan told me. I was overjoyed to think that I had had a place in his affections—he who could show such intense love for Our Lord.

"Every night I remember this as I say a prayer to Matt. I say my prayers from his small prayerbook, *The Little Treasury of Leaflets*. Susan gave it to me along with other books that belonged to him, before she died."

Speaking of Matt's chains, she said, "He always discarded the chains he wore when they became old and worn and smooth. The new ones, it seems, were rougher to his skin and he preferred that. I used to have two links of the chains he wore," she added, "but I gave them to two clergymen friends who were very interested in Matt's Cause.

"His sister, Susan Fylan, told me of a party he was at one night in the neighbourhood when he was a boy of sixteen," Miss Doyle recollected, gazing dreamily back through the years. "It was a merry affair with plenty of drink. Young Matt and his pal had been drinking for some time. Casting their eyes over the store of drink, they saw that there were only a few bottles left. So, they decided to get some more before the public houses shut. At the same time they didn't want to be seen leaving for that purpose. The noisy crowd was in a bunch in the middle of the floor, dancing, so Matt

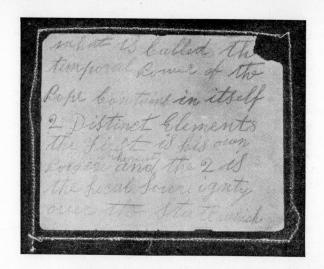

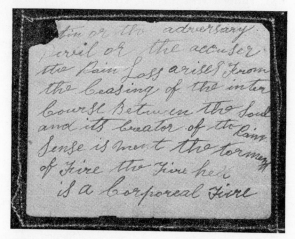

Specimens of Matt's handwriting. The two fragments are passages he copied from books he read. One reads: "The pain of loss arises from the ceasing of the intercourse between the soul and its Creator. By the pain of sense is meant the torment of fire. The fire of hell is a corporeal fire." The other reads: "What is called the temporal power of the Pope contains in itself two distinct elements. The first is his own inherent power and the second is the local sovereignty over the State which . . ." These are now in the Matt Talbot Legion Museum in Englewood, N. J.

said to his pal: 'I don't know how *you're* going to get out, but I know how *I'm* going out!' Down he dropped on his knees and crawled round the crowd until he came to the door and then he made down the stairs for all he was worth.

"Years afterwards," Miss Doyle added, smiling sadly, "when he had conquered this habit that surely would have brought on his downfall, he told Susan: 'Susan,' he said, never be too hard on the man who can't give up drink. For it's as hard to give up drink as it is to raise the dead to life again. But both are possible and even easy for Our Lord. We have only to depend on Him in constant prayers."

At this point, Mrs. Purcell said, "Miss Doyle wants to have a part in the work you are going to do for our Matt in America, Father. And she has brought two of Matt's books for you." (Of course Mrs. Purcell had arranged all that beforehand.)

Miss Doyle then gave me the books. One was a prayerbook entitled *First Steps to Heaven,* published in 1900. The other was a religious book entitled *The Practise of the Love of God,* published in 1823. On Page 3 and Page 60 of this second book, there is Matt's handwriting. His name is written on Page 3. On Page 60, he had written, "The 18th of August is the Feast of St. Joachim, the Father of the Blessed Virgin." Photos of these books are on Page 58.

Miss Doyle and Mrs. Purcell then drew up the following statement:

To Whom It May Concern:

I have today given to Father Albert Dolan, O. Carm., two books that belonged to Matt Talbot, one *First Steps to Heaven,* the other *The Practise of the Love of God* with Matt's own handwriting on Page 3 and Page 60. These books were given to me by Matt's sister, my first cousin.

(Signed) *Martha Doyle*
(Witnessed) *S. Purcell*

Under the circumstances, and in view of Mrs. Purcell's advance arrangements, I didn't know which of the ladies to thank, but I did my best to thank them both.

# 12.

## *Visit with Miss Kate Byrne*

IN my life of Matt Talbot, *Matt Talbot, Alcoholic,* there occurs this passage:

"After Mass every morning, Matt had to hurry to reach his work at six, but he always took time to fondle a beautiful collie dog which lay in the vestibule waiting for his mistress who was in church. It was through this dog that the lady made Matt's acquaintance and she gives us this revealing account of a visit she paid him:

"I called at his room in 1924, on a Saturday afternoon about three. He received me with great courtesy and set a chair for me near his fire. I was accompanied by my dog which he insisted on allowing into the room, saying he was very fond of dogs. We spoke first of his health which had broken the previous year and which explains his presence at home rather than at church on a Saturday afternoon. After a little time he changed the conversation to religious topics. He spoke of the Gospels, of Our Lady in particular, as he had great devotion to her, and of the various saints. I was entranced with his conversation and did not realize how long I had been listening until I saw by the clock that it was six. I had been listening to him for three hours, though I would not have believed I was there for more than half an hour. His room was poor but very clean and tidy. As I apologized for my long stay, his face lit up with pleasure and he thanked me warmly for my visit."

Upon my arrival in Dublin, I did not know this lady's name nor address. Neither Sir Joseph Glynn nor Father O'Donnell could help me in the matter. Mrs. Purcell had heard of the lady and assured me that the lady was still

*Above.* Father Dolan stands before the "pub" frequented by Matt Talbot before his pledge. *Left.* Father Dolan photographed at the corner of Newcombe Avenue and North Strand, where Matt Talbot stood the morning his friends passed him without inviting him to drink with them. *Below.* Holy Cross College, Clonliffe, where Matt took the pledge.

living but it took her several days to locate her. Finally, she said to me one morning, "Yesterday, I found the lady you are seeking. Her name is Miss Kate Byrne. I have seen her and she expects you sometime today."

"I'll go immediately," I said "and I wish you'd go with me."

On the way, Mrs. Purcell said of Miss Byrne: "She was an aristocrat once, very wealthy; she has come down a lot in recent years, but she's not poor."

We found Miss Byrne in a comfortable enough home and when we walked into her room, there she was sitting with a dog in her lap. (See photo, Page 39.) As we talked she kept her rosary twined about her fingers, just as Matt's mother is described as "rosary ever in hand."

Miss Byrne is a voluble old lady nearly 80 years of age. She told us how she first met Matt. "I found him in the church vestibule petting my dog, who jumped up on me as I approached. 'Is that yours?' said Matt, 'I talk to him every morning; he's a lovely dog.' Later that same morning a friend who saw me talking to Matt said 'You were talking to a saint.'

"When I missed him in church for several mornings, I inquired and discovered that he was ill and in Misericordia Hospital. I brought food to him there, fruit and delicacies. (Sister Dolores later was to mention this.) In the hospital, Mr. Talbot (I always called him "Mr. Talbot," never "Matt") introduced me to his two sisters, Mrs. Fylan and Mrs. Andrews. After he had left the hospital and returned, still in a weakened condition, to his room on Upper Rutland Street, I used to call on him with a little present of eggs, which I asked him to beat up and eat.

"I noticed that his bed was very flat and was covered with a dark quilt which covered pillow and all. I did not know then of course that he slept on planks and used a log for a pillow.

"In one of my visits, he told me that he had read, in the life of a saint, that he never got up from his knees in church lest he should be distracted. Mr. Talbot said with a little smile, 'That's why I don't stand up either.' "

Miss Byrne had been called by the Archbishop in 1931,

71

she told us, to be a witness at the Diocesan Inquiry into the virtues of Matt Talbot. As we talked she told us this none-too-clear story of Matt's power of prayer and prophecy, adding that she had forgotten to tell the story at the Process: "My sister's husband had been pensioned out of his job. My sister said to me, 'Will you ask Matt Talbot for something I want?' So I went to him before Mass in church and said: 'Mr. Talbot, may I speak to you?' 'You may.' 'Will you do something for a friend of mine?' 'I will;' and I explained that if my sister's husband continued to be pensioned out of his job, he'd have to go to London to work and that my sister did not want him to go. 'I hope he'll not have to go' said Matt Talbot. 'Your brother-in-law will get something,' he said positively. 'He'll be all right.'

"That very evening a telegram came to my brother-in-law. The telegram read, 'In the morning see the manager.' In the morning the manager told him that he was to continue on the job at full salary."

After Miss Byrne had graciously posed for pictures with us, we left, happy over our good fortune in speaking to one who had known Matt so well.

# 13.

## *Mrs. Annie Sweeney, Guardian and Tenant of Matt Talbot's Room*

IN JUNE, 1947 before I had made any definite plans to visit Dublin, one of the Mothers of the Sacred Heart Convent in Dublin sent me a clipping from the June 20th issue of *The Irish Independent*. It was an article signed "A. Sweeney" and was entitled *The Room Where Matt Talbot Lived*. Sir Joseph Glynn identified the author for me as Mrs. Annie Sweeney and gave me her address. But before I could manage to get out to the Sweeney home, Mrs. Purcell had invited her to meet Father Ronald and me at the Granby Lane Mission.

Mrs. Sweeney, the mother of sixteen children, is now 44. She has jet black hair; there is not a line in her face; she has a very quiet manner and voice, and impressed us by her complete calm and composure.

When I asked about her children's names, she answered: "Well, I have Theresa; I have Ignatius; I have Francis; I have Matthew; I have Dominic; I have Bernardette; I have Joseph; I have Mary . . . "I couldn't suppress a smile as I wrote the names. I missed some, but those I caught will give you the idea. Mrs. Sweeney is a grand character, thoroughly religious, sensibly pious, and imbued with the most tender devotion to Matt Talbot. She is in every way fitted to have been so long the guardian and custodian of Matt Talbot's room, sanctified by his prayers and penances. I'll let her tell her own story, as she told it to me:

"Two weeks after Matt Talbot's death in June 1925, I rented and occupied his humble tenement room. There were thirty applications for the room but I was the fortunate one, thank God. I moved into it with my husband and three child-

Matt Talbot's sisters. Mrs. Susan Fylan, left, died in 1941. Mrs. Mary Andrews, right, died in 1934. Photo taken at the Dublin Eucharistic Congress in 1932.

ren. Later when the family increased we were to rent other rooms adjoining Matt's, but at that time we all lived in his room.

"In his room, when we first moved in, I found in one of the two cupboards two old rosaries worn from continued use, some medals and small religious pictures, many of which I still possess. On his wall, there was the track of his big crucifix. The cross and all Matt's books and other belongings had been removed by his sisters, Mrs. Andrews and Mrs. Fylan, with both of whom I became close friends in the years to follow. In fact they gave me later one of his prayerbooks, and a link of his chains."

At this juncture, she opened the large semi-valise, which she had brought with her to Mrs. Purcell's shop, and showed me Matt's prayerbook, and the link of his chains.

She continued, "I was very happy in Matt's room for the ten years of my tenancy. But in 1935 because of the small space and a growing family, I had to move to a roomier home. I had tried to keep the children out of Matt's room, which I considered should be kept sacred, but it was impossible to have eyes for all of them all the time. Moreover the constant stream of visitors was too much for me as my family increased.

"Matt's room always possessed a marvelous spiritual atmosphere, as if one were kneeling at Benediction, and many

74

hundreds of priests and nuns, one Cardinal and some Bishops told me that they had the same feeling as they knelt there.

"So I regretfully left his room in 1935. Since then the room where Matt lived and sanctified himself has been locked up to preserve it from the thousands who would probably have wrecked the place by taking away pieces of the boards and shelves as Relics. At least, such was my experience for ten years, and it was only with the greatest watchfulness that I managed to preserve the room in the same condition as Matt left it. With the permission of his sister Mrs. Andrews, I did take with me, when I left, some Relics of the room for myself."

Here she reached again into the semi-valise and produced a number of articles all wrapped in cellophane.

"This," she said, "is a board from his cupboard, on which I found a few crumbs of food the day I moved into his room. This is the door knob or handle of his door, the inside knob which his holy hands grasped each day. This is a piece of board from directly beneath his crucifix; on this board he used to kneel for his hours of prayer. Mrs. Purcell told me, Father, that you are greatly devoted to Matt; so I brought these things with me to show you, especially since she tells me that you have written so much of the Little Flower, my favorite saint."

There she was again, the omnipresent St. Therese!

I thanked Mrs. Sweeney for lugging that heavy bag across Dublin for my sake, and I offered to take her home in a taxi. But she refused; the bus took her to her door, she said, and besides the neighbors would think lots of things if she came to her home in a taxi.

"I have more little things, Father, that belonged to Matt," she said, "which I'd like to show you if you'd visit my humble home, and I'd like you to meet the children."

So I made an appointment to visit her the next day. Before I left, I called Mrs. Purcell aside and whispered to her, "I can't bring myself to ask her to part with any of her Relics. She's so manifestly attached to them. I'd feel as if I were robbing her."

"If you were to rob her," Mrs. Purcell said, "you'd be a holy thief. In fact, Father, that's what I call you in my own mind; 'a holy thief.' But I'll help you. I've already told her you'd ask for some of her Relics. She knew that when she brought them here."

"You're a grand team-mate, Mrs. Purcell," I said, and then turning to Mrs. Sweeney, I asked, " Will you, Mrs. Sweeney, let Mrs. Purcell help you to make up your mind which of those Relics you're to give tomorrow to our Matt Talbot Legion in America? My heart is set at least on the door knob. But we'll talk it over tomorrow."

I left feeling that Mrs. Sweeney was in good hands in the company of my friend Mrs. Purcell.

The next day at the time appointed I arrived at the home of Mrs. Sweeney. It was a small, two-story, four-room cottage. The small yard and the house swarmed with children, to whom Mrs. Sweeney introduced me, one by one. They were well mannered, well behaved children and after they left to play, I said to Mrs. Sweeney, "You seem to have perfect discipline over the children."

"Oh, I have to," she said, "there would be no order if I didn't put my foot down."

"But you're so calm and quiet in your management of them."

"I have to be calm to get things done. I have to be washin' and sewin' after them and can't afford to lose energy by tempers. Matt and St. Therese both help me to be calm and patient."

"How many of your sixteen children are still living?"

"Fourteen; God took only two, blessed be His Holy Will. The mother of St. Therese lost four of her nine children in their babyhood; and she in my opinion was a saint. I, on the contrary, have lost only two of sixteen."

"Did you see," she asked, "the plaque of St. Therese, as you entered our home?"

"I did of course. How could any one miss it?" It was on the wall two feet from the door and I had seen it the minute the door opened.

"I bought that plaque," she said, "in 1925, shortly after I moved into Matt's room and it hung there in his room for ten years. Would you like to hold it?"

She took it from the wall and handed it to me, and dur-

*Top.* Father Dolan with Mrs. Sweeney and twelve of her sixteen children. Father Dolan is holding the plaque representing St. Therese, mentioned on page 76. *Bottom.* Father Dolan with Mrs. Sweeney.

ing my third visit with her later had me photographed with it. (See photo, Page 77.)

Then Mrs. Sweeney led me upstairs where in one of the two rooms she had a crude but touching Shrine. On a shelf there were the statues of Our Lord, Our Blessed Mother and St. Therese. Below them was a small picture of Matt Talbot. She had a vigil light burning before the Shrine. On the wall there was a large picture of Cardinal Verdier, Archbishop of Paris, perhaps the most distinguished of all visitors to Matt Talbot's room. The Cardinal visited the room at 18 Upper Rutland Street in 1932, during the Eucharistic Congress. Mrs. Sweeney was very proud of the Cardinal's visit and of the prayer the Cardinal had written on the occasion of his visit. She had framed the Cardinal's words and hung them beneath his picture. The words of his prayer were: "It is with profound emotion that I visited the place where the pious servant of God, Matt Talbot, lived and sanctified himself. May that Holy Worker help us to bring back to Christ our dechristianized people. That would be a new service which the dear Church of Ireland would render the world."

She also had framed a newspaper clipping describing the visit. The clipping reads:

"A Prince of the Church Walks Amongst the Poor of Dublin"

"Yesterday will live long in the minds and hearts of the poor of Upper Rutland Street and Granby Lane, as the Cardinal Archbishop of Paris came in his scarlet to make pilgrimage to the spot where Matt Talbot died and to the room where Matt lived. In Matt's room the Cardinal knelt and prayed for fully ten minutes, and then he blessed particularly Matt's sister, Mrs. Andrews, and the custodian of Matt's room, Mrs. Sweeney."

After I had knelt to say a short prayer there at Mrs. Sweeney's Shrine, she opened a drawer in the bureau and, without any preliminary, handed to me the door knob of Matt's room, the link of his chain, a candlestick from his mantel, a portion of the shelf of his cupboard and a piece of the plank from the floor of his room directly under the crucifix, the exact plank upon which he had always knelt.

"These", Mrs. Sweeney said, "are my gifts to The Matt Talbot Legion in America, and I will pray that all who see these Relics will be brought closer to Matt and will imitate his holiness."

"Mrs. Sweeney," I said, "are you sure you want to part with these treasures?"

"I don't," she declared, "but greater than my desire to keep them is my wish that many Americans may by seeing them come to know and love Matt better. Besides, I have still some little Relics of him to keep here. I have his prayer-book but I'd be glad to let you take some pages from it. What pages would you prefer?"

She removed four pages for me and four for Father Ronald and gave them to us as blithely as if she were the recipient and we the donors. I hope my readers will remember Mrs. Sweeney and her large family in their prayers.*

We returned then to the living room downstairs. I had a question or two which I had not yet had a chance to propose.

"You did not know Matt Talbot, is that correct?" I asked.

"I did not know him to speak to, but I knew him by sight. As a girl in my teens I lived quite near him. I used to see him walk past our house; he was not slovenly in his clothes which were old but not exactly shabby. He never raised his eyes as he walked. I used to pass him on the street, but he never noticed me. The only ones he'd notice were the children, with one exception. I remember that near us there was an old blind lady, who always sat on her front steps, smoking a pipe. As Matt passed her, he would always slip a pinch of tobacco to her. We children called him 'Mr. Talbot'; I used to see a priest pass our house and go into 18 Upper Rutland Street, and I said to mother, 'Who is that priest and who does he go to see?' She replied "That's Monsignor Hickey,† Mr. Talbot's friend; they talk and pray together.' "

---

*As I write this, a letter has come from Mrs. Sweeney in which she says, "The entire family recites each evening the prayer for Matt's canonization, and for the members of The Matt Talbot Legion, and for alcoholics."

†Unfortunately, Monsignor Hickey who knew Matt so well predeceased Matt and left us no information concerning him.

I said, "Mrs. Sweeney, you haven't told us much about your ten years in Matt's room. Isn't there more of interest that you remember?"

She talked on then in her quiet way as I took down what she said. "The most remarkable experience of my tenancy in Matt's room was to see many priests and people kneel and kiss the tenement floor boards where Matt knelt and prayed.

"In this connection I remember a priest from Holland who used to come every year to pray in Matt's room. One day I told him that before I rented the room, some one had thrown away the old gas jet that used to come down from the ceiling to Matt's table for his reading. The priest said 'What a pity. I'd give anything for a piece of it.' It was touching to see the devotion so many priests had for him. Many declared that Matt was a second St. Joseph.

"One day a lady came to me in Matt's room and told me this story about her daughter. It seems that Matt once met in Granby Lane this lady and her daughter, who had golden curls. Matt stopped and admired the little girl and made a complimentary remark about her curls. Her mother said 'They'll have to be cut off soon; the fashion, you know.' Matt said, 'Sometimes it's better to ignore the fashion; heaven is more important.' The child, the mother told me, is now a nun.

"On one occasion, a woman came to me in Matt's room for advice. She told me that once when she was about to be evicted, she went to Matt in his room for help. When she knocked at the door, Matt opened it and said, quick and cross, for she had probably interrupted his devotions, 'What is it?' She showed Matt the eviction notice and Matt asked, 'Have you children'? 'I have five' she replied. Matt then gave her the rent, thirty shillings. 'When do I have to pay it back?' she asked. Matt said 'When you can. Go on now.' The lady said 'I never paid it back to him, and now my conscience bothers me; what shall I do?' I told her that any priest would tell her that Matt being dead she should give it to the poor, which I hope she did.

"I forgot to tell you, Father, that I have a piece of the

banister just outside Matt's door to give you. Let me get it and I'll tell you the story of it."

She returned with the wood from the banister, and gave it to me and continued, "This piece of banister was always loose and his sister used to say it was because Matt banged it with his fist one day under these circumstances. It seems that after his mother died, his sisters discovered that in her insurance policy her age was stated as some years younger than she really was. Whose mistake it was, no one knew. But if her age had been stated correctly, the family would have received some pounds less from the policy. Matt's sisters wanted him to sign. Matt refused. The sisters continued to urge him and Matt banged the banister with his fist and said 'To sign would be a lie. And I'll be long enough in purgatory without a lie. I won't sign.' "

"Do you teach your children to be that honest, Mrs. Sweeney?" I asked.

"I do," she answered promptly, "but the children nowadays are not as easy to teach as when I was a child. I don't think it will be true of my girls, but I know lots of women now who grumble if they have only two or three children. I don't know what's got into the girls nowadays. I hear that some drink in public houses. The war did it. Our Irish girls brought it from England. Hundreds of Irish girls even now want to go to England. No, it's not the wages; it's the gaiety. They write for a couple of months and then there's a silence. And if they return here, they want to go back fast. I forbid my girls even to mention going to England. I tell them 'Stay in Catholic Ireland. Your faith comes first, not last.' I see to it that my boys and girls go to Holy Communion with their sodalities. I don't think I'll have any trouble with them. They won't want to travel to England and I wouldn't mind if they travel all they can afford in Ireland. I never travelled in my life; I don't even know my own country, for I always had two babies to look after. But it didn't hurt me, thank God, and they're grand children and a great blessing."

God give us more mothers like Mrs. Sweeney.

She then showed me her souvenir book which is a kind

of register in which she had visitors to Matt's room write their names and addresses. She had pasted on its cover this title: *My Ten Years in Matt Talbot's Room*. She told me I could take it and return it when I came, as she had asked, to photograph all the children. This photo was to be taken on a Saturday afternoon when all the older children would be home from work. When we came that Saturday, the scrubbing of faces was still in progress, as all fourteen Sweeneys prepared to be photographed with their mother and the priests from America. (See Photo Page 77.)

I can close this chapter about Mrs. Sweeney, the kind benefactor of The Matt Talbot Legion, in no better way than by recording what was in her "souvenir book" besides the names of prelates, priests and people from New Zealand, Holland, South Africa, Belgium, India, Canada, United States and Australia. On one page she had written this simple prayer "Matt Talbot, model of humility, pray for me and my family." On another page she had pasted a clipping which records the words of the Holy Father to a mother of twelve. I copied the words and here they are:

The Pope said to the mother of twelve, "You must be well content with this fact because it means that twelve times the Lord has had such faith in you that He has entrusted you with a new soul, a new life. When Christ calls a mother to the sublime office of maternity, He chooses her to cooperate in the solemn work of giving existence to a new soul, to a new life."

# 14.

## *Matt Talbot's Room*

AFTER a chapter devoted to the tenant and custodian of Matt Talbot's room, it is logical to follow with a description of the room itself.

Matt's room at 18 Upper Rutland Street is in one of the poorer tenement districts of Dublin. Photographs of the exterior of the building and of the room itself appear on Page 18 of this book.

It is a room about sixteen feet by ten, with two cupboards. All the furniture that Matt used (his bed, wooden planks and log pillow, and table), and all his belongings (books, crucifix, notes from his reading, clothing) were removed after his death by his sisters, Mrs. Andrews and Mrs. Fylan. Matt's two sisters, as we have seen and will see further, distributed much of his furniture and belongings to their intimate friends like Mrs. Purcell and Mrs. Sweeney. Eventually some of his furniture and belongings came into the hands of the Archbishop and of the Vice-Postulator of the Cause.

At present there are in the room the following articles: A replica of his original iron bed; a crucifix which resembles not too closely the one which belonged to Matt and which Father O'Donnell now possesses; a picture of Cardinal Verdier who visited the room in 1932; a prie-dieu or kneeler for the use of visitors; and a small table on which there is a Visitors' Register. On the prie-dieu there is a copy of the prayer for Matt Talbot's canonization. In a case, there are translations of Sir Joseph Glynn's original *Life of Matt Talbot* into Italian, Lithuanian, French, Austrian, Dutch, Hungarian, Maltese and Polish.

But even though the room has been stripped of Matt's possessions, it is still his room, and, as Mrs. Sweeney put it,

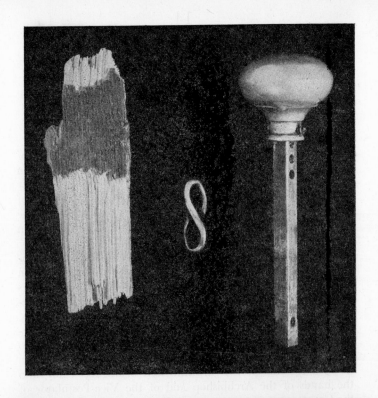

*Above.* Left to right: Portion of Matt's wooden pillow, a link of his chains, the door knob of his room. These are now in The Matt Talbot Legion Museum in Englewood, N. J. *Below.* Workmen who knew Matt Talbot and their employer. Left to right: Fuller; Thomas Martin, now head of the firm of T. & C. Martin Co.; Daly; Father Dolan; and Carew.

"The room is permeated with a distinctly spiritual atmosphere." While standing or kneeling in it, it is impossible to forget what took place here. As our Holy Father declared in his Decree introducing Matt's Cause: "This Servant of God undertook a form of advanced spiritual life that, especially in a workman, can scarcely be conceived."

It was here in this room that, on his knees, he sought the company of his borrowed religious books. It was here that he prayed for long hours of the night. It was here that he fasted; here that he partook of his frugal morning and evening meal; here that he performed his penances and took the few hours sleep that he permitted himself. It was here that, in the first months of his conversion, he fought the drink demon in his blood and conquered with the help of his constant prayers to Our Blessed Mother.

I don't believe, as I said to Father Ronald when we were leaving the room, that I ever said the prayer for Matt's canonization so fervently as I said it kneeling on the priedieu of his room. Father Ronald answered, "I feel the same way."

"We are leaving his room," Father Ronald said as we walked down the stairs, "but on account of the kindness of all who have given us Relics we really are taking with us to America a goodly portion of his room and belongings." Neither he nor I knew then how much more true that remark would be before we left Dublin.

# 15.

## *Mrs. Susan Byrne and Family;*

## *Matt's Iron Bed*

THROUGHOUT my visits with Matt's friends and relatives there was one question I kept repeating: "Where is his iron bed?" Some had no idea. Others said, "The Archbishop has it." But the Archbishop had told me that was the one article which the family had refused to give up.

There remained on my list just one other relative to visit, Mrs. Susan Byrne. She was Matt's sister's daughter. Her mother was the Mrs. Mary Andrews who has appeared so often in these pages. I had inquired about Mrs. Byrne from several who assured me that, although a close relative of Matt, she knew little about him. Consequently I kept postponing my visit to her home. It was to prove a very important and fruitful interview.

I had difficulty in finding her. I arrived at the address given me but the address proved to be that of a tobacco store. The proprietor knew no Mrs. Byrne. I and the taxi driver inquired in other adjoining stores. Finally we learned that the Byrnes lived in a room over the tobacco store. I climbed a steep, dark, rickety staircase, and at the top step, by lighting a match, I saw a door to my left. I knocked and the door was opened by a short, pleasant-faced lady who proved to be Mrs. Susan Byrne. I introduced myself and was in turn introduced to her children, James and Lily (Elizabeth) both in their late teens. The room in which they all lived had three beds and everything was neat and clean.

I said to Mrs. Byrne, "You are the daughter of the famous Mrs. Andrews, are you not?"

"Yes, my mother, Mrs. Andrews, was Matt Talbot's sister."

Mrs. Susan Byrne with her two children, James and Elizabeth, and
Father Dolan.

"Did you know Matt only through what your mother
told you or did you know him yourself?"

"Oh, I knew him when I was a girl and I saw him several times after I married. He kept to himself, you know,
most of the time, and even my mother did not see him
often."

"What do you remember best about him?"

"Whenever he talked to me, it was always about religion. I remember too that he didn't like to be disturbed
when he was at prayer in his room. He wouldn't refuse anyone anything they asked.

"Once when I was a young woman and was temporarily out of work I went to his room on Rutland Street and asked him to loan me two bob until I got a job. He gave it to me at once, saying to me, 'Don't forget now to give it back because that's money I put aside for the Chinese Missions'."

Mrs. Byrne is now fifty-seven years of age. We talked for a while of her mother. I said, "Mrs. Purcell, in Granby Lane, says your mother (Mrs. Andrews, Matt's sister) died in 1934. Others say it was 1935. Which is correct?"

"My mother died in 1934. Mrs. Purcell is right. She was a close friend of mother's. My aunt, Mrs. Fylan, died in 1941."

"I've been trying unsuccessfully to find an authentic picture of your mother and aunt. You wouldn't have a photograph of them, would you?"

She nodded affirmatively and went to the top drawer of a small bureau and gave me the photograph of Matt's sisters that is reproduced on Page 74. As some one remarked later when I showed the pictures, "There is plenty of character and strength in those faces."

"There never was a photograph of Matt himself, was there?" I asked.

"No, not one. He wasn't a man to have his picture taken. My mother used to say my Jimmie bore a remarkable resemblance to Matt. So did Mrs. Fylan. And as he grows older I think his likeness to Matt increases."

Later Mrs. Byrne and her children were photographed with me and the reader will find Jimmie's likeness on Page 87.

Evidently she had told me all of the little she knew about Matt. The time had come for the routine question which I asked hopelessly: "Do you know who has Matt's iron bed?"

"I have it," she said quietly. "It's there in that corner."

She pointed to one of the three beds in the room. The one she pointed out as Matt's was made up, as were the others, with mattress, pillows, coverlet.

"It's in use?" I asked doubtfully.

"Yes, Jimmie sleeps in it now."

"But that bed is a holy thing," I protested.

"Very holy," she agreed. "My mother also died in it, not to speak of its use by Matt himself."

"May I see the bed itself?" I asked. Mrs. Byrne pulled back the mattress and coverings and lifted a cover which concealed the iron projection which formed the footboard of the bed, and thus Matt's bed of iron stood revealed. I touched it reverently.

"Did the Archbishop ever ask you for the bed?" I asked.

"No, never. The former Archbishop, Archbishop Byrne, asked my mother, Mrs. Andrews, for it. But she refused to give it up because she wanted to die in it. But no one has asked me for it since her death. She willed it to me. We are poor and have to use it; otherwise, I'd let no one use it."

I explained to her the purpose of my visit to Dublin; I described The Matt Talbot Legion and the Museum we intended to have at the Legion national offices. Then I added, "The bed should really be in some such place. It does not belong here. Don't you agree? It does not belong in a private home, but should be where thousands would eventually see it, and, seeing it, be brought closer to Matt whose property it was. If you'd give the bed to me, I'd guarantee that thousands will see it. Moreover the sight of it will serve to develop a sense of nearness to Matt and consequently a more personal devotion to him."

Mrs. Byrne looked first at Lily, then at Jimmie, then at me, and said, "I'd have to speak to my other relatives before giving it away."

"Why?" I asked, "You've said you own it." I had visions of interminable family conferences, lasting beyond the day our plane would take off, and the bed still in the one-room Byrne home.

"I said, "You know, these family consultations develop only trouble and bad feelings. If I were you, I'd discuss it only with Jimmie and Lily. Then you can let me know your decision. Jimmie can bring me the word at the hotel tonight. Will that be all right?"

They all agreed and I asked Jimmie to accompany me downstairs. I gave him the address of the hotel and the

Father Ronald and Father Dolan photographed with Matt Talbot's Iron Bed. The bed is now in The Matt Talbot Legion Museum, Englewood, N. J.

room number and we fixed eight o'clock as the time he was to come. I asked him to do what he could to persuade his mother to a favorable decision.

"I've half a mind," I said, "to get Mrs. Purcell to talk with your mother. She seems to admire Mrs. Purcell."

"Oh, that won't be necessary," Jimmie replied, "mother'll give you the bed, I'm sure. No one sees it where it is. I often thought we shouldn't keep it."

"There's one thing I couldn't tell your mother, Jimmie, which I wish you'd tell her. I know you're not rich and I would naturally expect to replace the bed. You won't have to sleep on the floor."

When I returned to the hotel, I said to Father Ronald, "I have found Matt Talbot's bed. His sister's daughter has it. I think she's going to give it to us. Say a prayer to St. Therese and Matt that she will."

Promptly at eight o'clock that night, Jimmie presented himself at the hotel, dressed in his Sunday best. I had had a bad day, wondering what their decision would be and whether we were really to have that treasure or not, and I could scarcely wait for Jimmie to get seated.

He didn't keep me waiting, but said, as I took his hat, "Mother has decided to give you Matt's bed."

It seemed too good to be true. I breathed a prayer of thanksgiving. I wanted to shout in my exultation, but of course I had to be calm exteriorly.

"Thanks, Jimmie, for your part in the decision," I said. "Of course, we'll need a signed statement from your mother, giving the history of the bed. I'll tell you just about how it should read, incorporating what she told me this morning, and you can tell her, and she can have it ready for me to-morrow morning. Also because I have so little time left in Dublin, it will be necessary for us to move fast. I'll come to-morrow morning for the bed, so that I can have it crated for shipment. Will you unscrew the four bolts that I noticed hold the bed together, so that when I come, the bed will be ready for removal?"

When Father Ronald came in shortly after Jimmie's departure, I told him that the bed was ours.

"No!" he exclaimed. "It doesn't seem possible. After the Archbishop being refused it too! Are you going to tell him we have it?"

"I'll tell nobody we have it until it's well on its way to America. How we'll handle it I'll decide when I actually have possession of it. They may change their minds overnight."

Early the next morning after Mass, Father Ronald and I set out in two taxis, because one taxi would not hold the entire bed and because we needed the two drivers to help carry the bed, its weight, at a guess, being over one hundred pounds.

"Will you wait with the two drivers?" I said to Father Ronald, "while I go up to the Byrne room? If all is well, I'll call down to you from the window."

As I mounted that narrow, dark stairway again, I wondered whether the bed could be squeezed through it or whether it would have to be lowered from the window. Jimmie was waiting for me and had extracted the bolts and taken the bed apart. I gave the signal from the window and shortly the bed was on its way.

I handed to Mrs. Byrne an envelope that contained far more than enough to replace the bed and she handed to me her signed statement which reads:

To Whom it May Concern:

This iron bed which, to promote Matt Talbot's Cause in America, I have given today to Father Albert Dolan, first belonged to Matt's mother, Mrs. Talbot, my grandmother. Then it became the property of Matt Talbot, and after his death, passed into the possession of my mother, Mrs. Andrews, Matt's sister. In it my mother died, after which the bed became mine.

(Signed) *Mrs. Susan Byrne*

Before leaving I said to Mrs. Byrne, "I'm so breathless that I can't thank you properly now. But I'll see you all again this afternoon when I come with the photographer. I'll try then to thank you adequately." I hope I succeeded, and I hope Jimmie sleeps well every night in his new bed.

Matt's bed couldn't be brought to the hotel. What to do with it? We could hardly ask the Archbishop to retain it in safe keeping for us. An old-fashioned iron bed, which was made when folding beds were not yet invented, is not the easiest article in the world to find a place for, even temporarily. We decided to bring it to the home of friends of ours in Dublin, the Cassidy family. When Mrs. Cassidy saw the iron bed being carried in, she took a fit of laughter. But when she learned that it was really Matt Talbot's bed, she wanted it put together so that her daughter who had been ill could sleep in it that night. At the Cassidy's the bed was crated and subsequently shipped to us.

# 16.

## *Sister Dolores and Sister Ignatius*

MY LIST of people who had known Matt Talbot and whom I was to try to interview was getting short. Left on the list was Sister Ignatius who received Matt's body at Jervis Street Hospital the morning he died, and Sister Dolores who had had charge of the ward in Misericordia Hospital while Matt was there as a patient for six weeks, two years before his death. Both Sisters had been witnesses at the Process.

We had been able to get no information from those with whom we had talked as to whether these Sisters were still living or not. So we decided to ask at the Hospital itself, and since Jervis Street hospital was the nearer, we went there first. There we were told that Sister Ignatius was indeed alive and still on active duty. She was sent for and came to the visitors' parlor where Father Ronald and I had been taken.

She is an Irish Sister of Mercy, aged but ageless. She brightened when we told her that we came in the interests of Matt Talbot's Cause. She was very willing to speak of him.

"I never knew him," she said, "and never saw him until the morning he was brought into our morgue here dead."

"Will you tell us just what happened that morning Sister?"

"His body was brought to the morgue in the Corporation Ambulance. His identity was unknown. His body was accompanied by a police officer whose name I never knew. (It was Officer Hanlon). I was called and went, with a nurse and a hospital porter, to prepare the body for burial. As I was cutting away the clothes from his arms, my scissors struck something hard. It was his chains. I didn't know what to make of it—whether he was a saint or what he was. In a

Sister Ignatius.

few minutes the porter also discovered chains binding his body around the waist. I remember the porter said, 'He's either a mad man or a saint.'

"At any rate we reverently removed the chains, which were rusty, but the body was scrupulously clean. We removed the chains to have the body ready for the inquest and post-mortem examination. But strange to say, there was no inquest. When we called the coroner, he decided 'No inquest,' and his decision struck me as strange then and still does. I still don't know why there was no inquest."

"How long was it, Sister, before he was identified?"

"It was the next morning. His two sisters, Mrs. Andrews and Mrs. Fylan, identified and claimed the body. He was buried from St. Francis Xavier's Church on Upper Gardiner Street on the Feast of Corpus Christi."

"Have you devotion to him, Sister?"

"I have indeed. I say prayers in his honor every morning at Mass. I don't ask him for favors, that is, except spiritual ones; and he doesn't fail me. I say daily the prayer for his canonization."

It was with reluctance that Sister Ignatius consented to be photographed. The photo did not prove to be a clear one but is reproduced on this page.

I asked her if Sister Dolores was alive and still at Misericordia Hospital. "She's alive," she answered, "but she's now at another hospital, St. Kevin's Hospital in the South Dublin Union."

Sister gave us directions and after being photographed outside the Jervis Street Hospital Mortuary where Matt's

Sister Dolores with Father Dolan.

body had been brought that June morning in 1925, we set out for St. Kevin's.

## Sister Dolores

When we arrived at St. Kevin's Hospital, we found that Sister Dolores was expecting us. Sister Ignatius had telephoned her that we were coming and warned her that we had a camera. "So I tidied up a bit", said Sister Dolores, who is a bright-eyed, rosy-cheeked, voluble, vivacious old lady. She was quite in contrast to Sister Ignatius who, although pleasant, was staid and dignified.

It should be said that in the parlour in which we talked to Sister Dolores, the Little Flower's picture looked down upon us.

Sister Dolores gave us her story without prompting and it resembles very closely the statement she made to Sir Joseph Glynn and at the Process. "Yes, I had charge of St. Lawrence's ward in Mater Misericordiae Hospital when Matt was there as a patient. He was there about six weeks; from the first of October to the middle of November, 1923.

"He remained in bed most of the time he was in the hospital. No, he did not then wear chains. He was very quiet and retiring and had little to say to anyone.

"He had a very sweet smile, and was always very gracious and courteous in his manner."

Here I interrupted to show her the paintings of Matt Talbot in general circulation. "Do they look anything like him?" I asked.

95

"They do, but he didn't look so sanctimonious. Matt Talbot was jovial, bright and cheerful. Those paintings miss his pleasant expression and his little smile."

She continued her story. "He took whatever food was given him without comment or complaint. I did notice that he did not take butter. His sisters and a Miss Byrne used to bring him eggs and fruit. These he handed to me but he'd never ask for them unless I reminded him. When Miss Byrne brought butter, he'd say to me afterwards 'Give it to the other patients, Sister.'

"He went to Holy Communion frequently, but I noticed that he was reluctant to ask the priest to come. He didn't want to bother anyone. But whenever I'd ask him if he wished to receive, he'd always agree.

"One day he had a bad heart attack, and I had him anointed, and sent for his sisters. I told them he was dying, and I remember I said to them, 'It is just as well that he die now, for he'll never be better prepared or have a happier death.' Of course I didn't know then that God had other plans and that it was to be through a public death on a public street, bound by his chains, that God was to make his life known to the world. If he had died then in the hospital, no one would ever have heard of him afterward.

"I was certain that day that he was dying. In fact for a few minutes I was sure that he was dead, for, after he had received Viaticum, he seemed not to breathe. I now think that it was his profound adoration of Our Lord after receiving Him in Viaticum that explains his death-like immobility.

"He recovered from this attack and after a few days was allowed up. The first day he was permitted to be out of bed he disappeared. The nurse reported to me, 'I can't find Mr. Talbot!' 'My goodness,' I said, 'he may have gone out and collapsed on the street. Look everywhere for him.'

"Just then the bell rang for the Sisters' chapel prayers and I went to the chapel and found him there in the corner of the chapel, praying. I said, 'You have given us a great fright.' He replied with his usual little smile, 'I have thanked the nurses and the doctors and I thought it only right to thank the Great Healer!'

"His words so impressed me that since then I've always

suggested to patients that they go to the chapel to thank Our Lord for their recovery.

"While he was in the hospital, I and several of the other Sisters noticed his complete absorption and profound recollection in the chapel. He was in the chapel every evening when the Sisters recited the Office. He was always in a remote corner and always kneeling erect.

"He did not speak of religious matters with the Nuns. Some patients like to discuss religion, but Matt Talbot never showed by his behavior or conversation that he was anything more than a sweet-natured, holy old man. Knowing now the life of austerity which he led, it is clear to me that he sought to conceal his holiness from all around him. I thought of him then just as a very holy old man, more like a Trappist monk than a workman."

"Do you pray to him, Sister?"

"I do of course, and with excellent results." Then she told us a story of her examination papers, her prayers to Matt at the time and her conviction that Matt was responsible for the success of her examination. Like Sister Ignatius, she assured us that she prays daily for his canonization.

She very cheerfully and willingly posed for her photograph which is reproduced on Page 95.

# 17.

## *Brother Furlong*

MATT TALBOT in his younger days seemed to prefer the Carmelite Church of St. Teresa on Clarendon Street. In his later years, he usually went for Mass to the less distant St. Francis Xavier's Church on Upper Gardiner Street. He was a member of the men's sodality of St. Francis Xavier's; it was this sodality that erected his tombstone, and it was from this church that he was buried.

The church opened at 5:30 A. M. but Matt usually arrived at the entrance about 5:00. While he waited for the church to open he knelt in prayer on the steps of the church. The Brother who, as Porter, opened the doors of the church every morning was Brother Furlong, who, I had heard, was still alive. I went to St. Francis Xavier's and asked whether Brother Furlong was still there. He was, but was out at the time. I then asked for the Director of the Men's Sodality instead. Father Charles Moloney, S. J., came to the parlor, and we had a long talk about Matt Talbot. Father Moloney never knew Matt but had acquired much information concerning him from Brother Furlong. Father Moloney had, however, known Father Murphy, S. J. who had been director of the Men's Sodality in Matt Talbot's time.

"Father Murphy used to say," said Father Moloney, 'Matt Talbot belongs to us, body and soul,' and he used to urge his Jesuit Superiors to claim Matt and to take up Matt's Cause, but because the Superiors never approved nor disapproved, no action was taken."

I explained to Father Moloney, who is a member and director of The Catholic Total Abstinence Union of Ireland, the scope and purpose of The Matt Talbot Legion in America. He was very much impressed, especially with our attempt to persuade not only total abstainers but all to help alcoholics. "Your Legion," he said "is far more inclusive than our Total Abstinence Union and such an organization as the Legion is needed here in Ireland as well as in the States. It is a grand goal you have set for yourselves: to help alcoholics."

I told him of my desire to get, first-hand, Brother Furlong's memories of Matt Talbot and to take his photograph. "I understand," I said, "that he's allergic to cameras."

"I'll see if I can persuade him," Father Moloney said. "Come, he should have returned by now." As he led me through the corridor to the Church, Father Moloney told me that Brother Furlong was still on active duty as Porter and Sacristan.

We found Brother Furlong in the sacristy and Father Moloney introduced me. Brother Furlong is a hale, hearty man whose appearance belies his age, sixty-nine.

"How long have you been here at St. Francis Xavier's, Brother?" I asked.

"Forty years this month," he answered, "I came here in 1907."

"You knew Matt Talbot?"

"Sure, I knew him. I knew him as 'Mr. Talbot.' Only those who knew him very well called him 'Matt.' I used to open the doors of the church for him every morning. He'd be the first in every morning, sun, rain or snow. As soon as I opened the door, he'd go up the middle aisle to the altar railing, genuflect on both knees to the Blessed Sacrament and then bend and kiss the floor. After a while, he'd go over to the extreme right end of the communion railing and leave his hat there. That was to secure his place, for he wanted to be first to receive Holy Communion, because he had to get to his work. After leaving his hat, we would then make the Stations of the Cross. After finishing the stations, he would kneel at the extreme right end of the rail where he received Holy Communion given then before Mass. Leaving the rail, he would kneel in an obscure corner of the church during Mass. He knelt erect, without any support whatever, his hands clasped in front of him, and his eyes shut. In this position he knelt for the entire period he was in the church. And on Sundays that was from early morning until 1:30

Brother Furlong and Father Dolan.

P. M. I knew I couldn't kneel that long; how he did it is a mystery to me.

"What I liked about him," continued Brother Furlong, "is that he never did anything to attract attention to himself. You'd have to be about the church all the time, as I was, or you'd not know as much about him as I did. I liked his quiet manner and his hidden way. Wasn't it a grand dispensation of Providence that after so hidden a life, he should die on a public road with his chains on him and thus become known?"

"Did you know about his chains while he was still living, Brother?"

"I did not. I never had the slightest inkling of them. He was a shy man. Unless he had business with me, he wouldn't speak to me unless he was addressed. He did not want to be a bother to anyone. At first when he'd give me money to give to the priests for charity, I'd say, 'Give it yourself to one of the priests,' but he'd answer, 'They are too busy to be bothered. Will you take care of it?' After a while, I got used to him."

Father Moloney then interposed a question. "Brother,"

he asked, "did Mr. Talbot go to confession to Father Murphy?" (Father Murphy, S. J. was, in Matt's time, director of the Irish Catholic Total Abstinence Union and with Matt's history Father Moloney expected that there would be contacts between them.)

"He did not," replied the Brother to Father Moloney's surprise. "There was a Monsignor Hickey who was Mr. Talbot's director. Matt liked Father Murphy, he told me, but he did not go to confession to him.

"I remember his giving some money to Father Murphy for the poor one day. Father Murphy took the bill and looked at it casually and a moment later saw that it was a five pound note. He turned to inquire the name of the donor but Mr. Talbot had disappeared."

"Did any of the priests here suspect Matt's holiness during Matt's life?" I asked the Brother.

"None of them knew him by name," replied the Brother. "But our Father Casey told me one day, 'There's a saint attending this church. I never saw any one receive Holy Communion with such fervor.' Father Casey did not know then who the man was. But after Matt's life was published, he questioned me and identified the man as Mr. Talbot by the first place he always had at the Communion rail."

"You were one of the few, weren't you, Brother," I asked "who knew that Matt had slit his trousers so that he'd kneel on his bare knees?"

"I was," said Brother, "but I'd never have noticed it if a woman had not seen it first and told me to look sharply and I'd see what she saw."

Then there followed an animated discussion as to whether Brother would be photographed, and with Father Moloney's assistance the Brother was persuaded, and the photograph of him which appears on Page 100 was taken.

# 18.

## *Visit to the Dublin Carmel*

I WENT to the Dublin Carmelite Convent to see there the original painting of Matt Talbot done by one of the Sisters there, Sister Cecilia. The Convent is far out of Dublin proper on the Tallaght Road. A high wall surrounds and hides the convent grounds. Being admitted by the secular gate-keeper, I walked to the convent entrance, obeyed the sign "Ring and Enter," and found myself in front of a small panel, the door of which was presently pulled aside. Through a screen in the panel, a voice said, "Thanks be to God."

I said "Sister, I am an American priest and have come here to see your famous painting of Matt Talbot, and if I may, to speak to the Sister who painted it."

"What is your name, Father?"

"Father Albert Dolan. I'm a Carmelite."

"Father Albert Dolan! We've read your Little Flower books in our refectory. I'll call the Sisters immediately. Will you go into the parlor; it is the room to your right."

I entered and sat before a grille which is almost exactly like the grille in the Carmel of Lisieux. Soon I heard voices behind the grille and then one voice saying, "Our Mother Superior has just died a month ago, Father, and we have not chosen another Superior yet, but I welcome you in the name of our community. We know you well, Father, through your books. We never thought to be visited by you. You are very welcome."

"Less than a week ago, Sister, I talked with the two living Sisters of St. Therese and they opened the grille."

There was a short consultation and the bolts were drawn, the panels of the grille opened, the curtains pulled back, and there were then revealed three Sisters in their Carmelite habits.

We had a grand time. There was at first no talk about Matt Talbot, for the Sisters wanted to know all about my latest visit to Lisieux. How was Mother Agnes, how was Sister Genevieve, what did they say and so on. The Dublin Carmel, I learned from them, is one hundred and twenty years old. There are only ten Sisters there because they can accomodate no more in the convent given to them more than a century ago. They are poor but gay and happy, the happiest Sisters I've ever met outside Lisieux.

Finally we commenced to discuss the purpose of my visit. One of the three Sisters was Sister Cecilia, who painted the picture of Matt Talbot that I'd come to see.

"How did you happen to paint his picture, Sister?" I asked.

"Well, at first, it was just a sketch I made out of my imagination. I used to make little sketches at recreation to amuse myself and the other Sisters. And Mrs. Fylan, Matt Talbot's sister, used to come here. She often spoke of Matt Talbot to us. From her description of him, I knew something of his appearance and made the sketch of him. Then our Reverend Mother, God have mercy upon her, thought I should make a painting of it. We are all very devoted to Matt here and one of our Sister's father knew him by sight, and another of our Sisters is a cousin of Raphael O'Callaghan, who knew Matt so well and who gave Sir Joseph Glynn so much information about Matt. So for all these reasons I completed the painting. I worked on it under the supervision of Mrs. Fylan. I arranged his tie just as she told me he wore it and drew his hands and beads according to her dictation. There was a Mr. Colligan also who helped some."

"Who was Mr. Colligan, Sister?"

"He was a workman who knew Matt Talbot well. He came here to ask for work, for he was in bad health and we gave him odd jobs for a while. Several times Reverend Mother had me show him the painting as I worked and he was kind enough to say it resembled Matt. Both Mr. Colligan and Mrs. Fylan agreed that Matt was a little man with a hair-line mustache and that's the way I tried to paint him. But if I got anything like Matt, it was only through prayer."

"The Archbishop and some others told me that, according to their information, your painting is more like Matt than any other painting. May I see the original, Sister?"

"We haven't the original, Father. A publisher came here one day and Reverend Mother sold it to him. But I have a large copy of the original; it is an exact duplicate. In fact, we have several. I'll let you see them, Father."

She passed three large copies of her painting of Matt to me. Two were colored, one in black and white. I had seen the picture often but never in so large a form. Sister Cecilia let me have the black and white copy for The Matt Talbot Legion Museum. I explained the Legion to the Sisters and then said to them, "I'm enrolling all of you as members of his Legion and I ask you to pray every day, as all members are asked to do, for alcoholics."

There was in answer a chorus of promises that they would so pray.

When I told them of my quest of Relics of Matt Talbot for the Legion Museum, the Sisters immediately offered to give and did give us their Relic of Matt, a piece of his wooden pillow several times larger in size than the one given us by the Archbishop.

"Do you pray to Matt Talbot here, Sisters?" I asked.

"Oh, we do," replied Sister Cecilia. "We pray to him and for him. We pray for his canonization and we make novenas to him."

"I must tell you, Father," continued Sister Cecilia, "that my brother who is a priest told me of being directed last year, through prayer to Matt Talbot, to the bedside of one who was dying and who would otherwise have died without the Sacraments."

The second Sister at the grille was Sister Mary of the Holy Ghost. She looked about twenty-one, but upon being asked, she told me that she had been a professed Carmelite for fourteen years. "My father," she said, "used to go to the same Mass as Matt in St. Francis Xavier's and if he arrived early before the church doors were opened, he would see a man kneeling on the church steps. When he read Matt's life, he said, 'That surely was the man I used to see kneeling outside the Gardiner Street Church.' "

The third Sister was Sister Teresa Evangela. She had

before coming to Carmel, once been a patient in Mater Misericordiae Hospital when Matt was a patient there, but she did not meet him or know him. She said, "Father, the Mr. Colligan we mentioned told us that Matt told him once, speaking of his conversion, 'I got the grace from God and I didn't look back.' Isn't that a lovely way of expressing it?"

"And, Father," she continued, "since you're seeking information about Matt, you should talk with Sister Barbara at St. Vincent's Hospital."

"I never heard of her, Sister. Did she know Matt?"

"No, but she had, as a patient, a workman who knew Matt and who said that Matt told him that he (Matt) never lost his craving for drink. Do you believe that, Father?"

"I don't know. It would seem that the craving would not last all those years. At most, it would return only rarely and not too vehemently. Yet, it could be, I suppose. What do you think, Sister?"

"We've talked of it, Father, and we think that maybe it was on account of the craving that he took to wearing the chains. Maybe that was to subdue his craving."

Sister Cecilia interposed, "But some of us think that his chains were not to subdue the body, which he had already conquered; we think that he wore the chains and practiced his austerities to help others and to make himself more like Our Crucified Lord. Which opinion do you think is correct, Father?"

"If my opinion is worth anything, I agree with you, Sister Cecilia. I'll send you the book *Matt Talbot, Alcoholic* in which I explain his austerities just as you have explained them. But I will contact Sister Barbara."

Since I had no time before leaving Dublin to visit Sister Barbara, Father Ronald went to see her. He reported that she did not know the name of the workman to whom Matt was supposed to have said, "I never lost the craving for drink." Neither was there any evidence, except the nameless workman's word, that Matt really made any such statement. Father Ronald also reported that Sister Barbara is most enthusiastic about Matt's Cause, and even annoyed at the delay in canonizing him. "She prays daily for his canonization," said Father Ronald, "and promised me to pray daily

105

for alcoholics and for the members of The Matt Talbot Legion."

But let us return to the Sisters at the Dublin Carmel. They had known Raphael O'Callaghan well because he used to visit his cousin there at Carmel. They repeated what Sir Joseph Glynn had told me, that Raphael was the man who loaned Matt theological books. The Sisters also said that Raphael had been ill for several months in 1925 and left his home for the first time on June 8 of that year. He met an acquaintance of Matt's that day and asked for Matt, saying "How is Matt? I've been ill and haven't seen him for nine months."

"He's just now dead" was the reply. "He died yesterday."

Raphael hurried to the Jervis Street hospital and was instrumental, the Sisters said, in arranging, with the Fathers of Gardiner Street, Matt's burial, thus saving him from a pauper's grave.

The hour grew late, too late for visitors at Carmel, I maintained. But the Sisters overruled me declaring that since I was a Carmelite and had come so far, it was permissible to make an exception. The conversation would drift from Matt Talbot to St. Therese and back again until I said, "Sisters, do you notice how we are linking Matt and the Little Flower?", and I described for them how omnipresent she had been throughout those days in Dublin.

"It is not surprising," declared Sister Cecilia, "for he was very devoted to her and copied with his own hand, I have read, the long prayer for her canonization. It was found in his prayerbook, as perhaps you know, after his death."

"Yes, Sister, I know. And you will all be glad to know that we have linked Matt and St. Therese together in The Matt Talbot Legion, for the principal Patrons of the Legion are the Holy Ghost, Our Blessed Mother and St. Therese."

The Sisters were delighted at this news, and renewed their promises to help the members of the Legion by their prayers.

I said, "It will be the part of your new Reverend Mother to remind the Community of that promise. And since you'll have your election soon, I'll predict that the new Superior will be Sister Cecilia."

I could tell from the pleased exclamations of the other two that Sister Cecilia was really their choice. If that event comes to pass, it will not be surprising, for Sister Cecilia is one of those very humble souls who are predestined to be exalted.*

When the Sisters knelt for my blessing, I knelt with them and asked their prayers, and as I was leaving the parlor, Sister Cecilia said, 'Don't forget, Father, to send us all your books."

I replied, "I won't forget. I'll address them to you, Sister and when you acknowledge them, you'll sign yourself. 'Mother Cecilia.' "

Their laughter, as I closed the door, was a fitting and musical termination of that pleasant and profitable visit to the Carmel of Dublin.

*A letter from the Dublin Carmel confirms the election of Sister Cecelia as Prioress.

# 19.

## *Visits with Irish Leaders: De Valera, O'Kelly, and the Papal Nuncio*

WE had reservations on a plane leaving Ireland for America on a Tuesday. On Sunday morning, Father O'Donnell, the Vice-Postulator of Matt Talbot's Cause, telephoned me. He said, "I forgot to tell you that the President of Ireland, the Honorable Sean T. O'Kelly, was a witness at Matt Talbot's Process. As a boy, he knew Matt. You ought to try to see him."

"How do I go about that?"

"Write him, explaining your mission to Ireland and your 'Matt Talbot Legion.' As President, he'll be interested in an American organization named after a native of Ireland. I think he'll see you."

"There's no time to write. I'm leaving Tuesday."

"Tuesday! Well, I guess we're too late. It's too bad I didn't tell you before about him."

Afterwards I pondered the project. It was a visit not to be missed without a try. There must be some way, even though time was running out, of arranging a visit with this head of a state who had known Matt Talbot. Finally I thought of our friends, the Cassidys, whom I had been forced to neglect because I had not had a free minute for social visits, and whose invitation to lunch that day I had been obliged to decline.

I said to Father Ronald, "Isn't Mr. Cassidy's work in some way connected with the Government?"

Father replied in the affirmative. So I asked, "Will you phone him and tell him that I find that I can after all accept his invitation to lunch today at his house?"

After lunch with Mr. and Mrs. Cassidy and their grand,

thoroughly Catholic family of eight children, I said to Mr. Cassidy, "Do you know any one close to President O'Kelly?"

"I do. I know his secretary. He visits us here three or four times a week."

Father Ronald and I exchanged smiles at our good fortune. It was but one of an unbroken series of fortunate coincidences that had followed us from the time we left America and caused us both to remark often, "Both St. Therese and Matt are at our side."

I explained to Mr. Cassidy my desire to meet the President, and asked him if it were possible to get his secretary on the phone on a Sunday.

"Perfectly possible. Unless he's in the country. I'll try now."

The President's secretary was soon on the wire and after Mr. Cassidy's preliminary explanation, the secretary asked to speak with me. He asked a dozen questions and then said, "In view of your departure Tuesday, I'll try to squeeze you in some time tomorrow. I'll call you back within an hour."

He was as good as his word and phoned that the President had fixed the appointment for 12:15 Monday noon.

There was general jubilation. Mr. Cassidy said "You'll see some lay-out. The President lives in Phoenix Park in the Vice-Regal Lodge, one of the finest buildings in Europe. It was Britain's last gift to Ireland, for England built the Lodge as the residence of the British Viceroys to Ireland."

"What pleases me," I said, " is the possibility of getting from the President a message to the members of The Matt Talbot Legion. That's important not only because he is President of Ireland but also because he knew Matt Talbot. I wonder how and when he knew him."

The next morning I asked Father Ronald not to forget to bring his camera just in case the President would consent to pose for a picture. Father Ronald said, "Will they let me in? The appointment was made for you."

"But I told the secretary there were two of us. We'll both get in somehow."

When our taxi arrived at the closed gates of the Vice-Regal Lodge, the car was stopped by the military. We were asked our names. The soldiers consulted a list, and one said,

"We have no instructions to admit Father Ronald, only Father Dolan."

I said, "That's just an oversight. Father Ronald is my companion. Let him come with me as far as the door anyway, and I'll see what can be done about it at the Lodge."

"I'll have to telephone," said the guard.

While he telephoned, Father Ronald said, "In view of all this formality, it doesn't look as if I'll get to use the camera. I can't see the President having his picture taken after all this."

"You're probably right. But 'a faint heart,' you know. We'll have a try at it."

When the soldier returned he said, "Father Ronald may go as far as the door," and he swung the gates open and we drove through surpassingly beautiful grounds to the Vice-Regal Lodge, a photograph of which is reproduced on Page 111.) There a tall officer met me as I entered the door. He took my hat and asked me to sign the register, an elaborately bound book in the hall. As I signed, I noticed that the day before one of the President's callers was Eamon de Valera.

The officer gravely conducted me into an inner waiting room with beautifully panelled ceilings and with a view of the inner gardens which, though less extensive, reminded me of the Vatican Gardens in Rome.

At precisely 12:15, another officer appeared and led me down a corridor a few steps into the President's office. As I entered, the President arose from his desk, stepped forward to shake my hand, and indicating a lounge opposite the desk as my seat, he sat beside me. The President is a short, affable gentleman of sixty-five, impeccably attired.

I briefly explained my mission and then said, "I understand, your Excellency, that you were a witness at the Process. You knew Matt Talbot?"

"Yes, when I was a boy, I served the early Mass at Matt's parish church, St. Joseph's on Berkeley Road. I lived then directly opposite the church. Matt Talbot often attended that early Mass, and since I often saw him at Mass and at Holy Communion, I was able to testify at the Process concerning his devotion and concerning his appearance."

*Top.* The Viceregal Lodge, residence of President O'Kelly. *Bottom.*
The Honorable Sean O'Kelly, President of Ireland, with Father Dolan.

"Do you mind repeating for me your memories of him?"

"Not at all. I was ten or eleven when I first saw Matt.
He was always there before the church opened. He would
kneel on the steps outside while he waited. I remember that
during the Mass, he used to kneel on the dark side of the
Church, the North side, near St. Joseph's altar. And we boys
used to notice that he prayed there with rapt fervor. He
didn't, as some do, just kneel there, occasionally looking
about, but knelt erect with his eyes shut and hands clasped
before his breast. He'd kneel that way motionless all during
Mass. We couldn't help but notice his extreme devotion."

"Did you ever speak to him?"

"No, never. I was a boy and he was then a man nearly
forty years of age. I saw him on the street often but more
often I saw him from the altar as I was serving."

111

" I have with me two paintings of him, Your Excellency. Would you mind telling me which is the more like him?"

The President selected Sister Cecilia's painting. "That is somewhat like him," he said, "but his expression is not pleasant enough. When he wasn't praying, he had a very attractive little smile. He was a small man, about my height."

I then explained the purposes of The Matt Talbot Legion and when the President expressed his enthusiasm over the project as I outlined it, I asked him for a message to the members of the Legion.

"Well," he said thoughtfully, " I'm not skilled in that kind of thing. But let this be my message: I am deeply impressed with the possibilities of your Legion and with the opportunities it presents for accomplishing wide-spread good for humanity, especially for alcoholics. I believe that the Legion will be good for alcoholics and good for those that help alcoholics. Its possibilities are tremendous."

Then we talked of less important things. He told me that he had known intimately our former Carmelite Prior General, Father Peter Magennis. The President remarked that while in America some years ago, he had visited our Englewood Shrine of St. Therese. (There she was again, the ever-present Little Flower.)

As I rose to go, I said, looking out over the Gardens. "You have a wonderfully beautiful place here in which to live."

"Yes," he smiled, pointing to the desk; "as I sit there, I often recall that that desk was intended really for the Viceroy of England. But now it is used by the President of Ireland."

"I wonder, Your Excellency, if I am being too bold in asking another favor. Your secretary didn't include, as I intended, my companion, Father Ronald, in this audience. The officers wouldn't admit him. He's outside and would like to meet you. Besides, he has a camera and maybe you wouldn't mind letting him take your picture."

"Surely, certainly," the President assented with smiling graciousness, "I'll go to the entrance with you."

To the manifest embarrassment of the guard, who followed at a distance, the President walked with me to the Lodge door, where I summoned Father Ronald and introduced him to the President. The pictures were taken (See

Page 111), and afterwards the President chatted leisurely with us. Pointing to a building in the distance, he said, "That's the residence of the Papal Nuncio, Archbishop Robinson. Have you seen him?"

"No, I had no idea he lived so near. Is he at home?"

"He is. He's having lunch with me today, which is my sixty-fifth birthday. Why don't you call on him? He'd be interested in your Legion."

"But would he see me without an appointment? May I say you sent me?"

"Yes, if you like. Hurry though, because he's due here for lunch shortly."

We hastily said our good-byes and were off for the Papal Nuncio's palace.

## The Papal Legate to Ireland, Archbishop Paschal Robinson

At the Palace, I went through the now familiar routine: first, an explanatory interview with the Italian Monsignor who is the Nuncio's secretary; then a considerable wait; then the return of Monsignor to say that the Archbishop would come shortly.

Archbishop Robinson, the Papal Legate to Ireland, is a feeble, kindly old man. "I have been ill," he said. "This is the first time I've been out since my illness. My secretary says you're a Carmelite from America. What's your mission here —something to do with Matt Talbot?"

I explained in detail. He followed my description of the Legion with vigorous nods of his venerable head and an occasional explosive "Splendid!" I asked him for a message to the members of the Legion.

He said, "Of course, I can give you nothing formally official. But you can say that I am deeply impressed with the laudable purpose of such an organization to help the unfortunate alcoholics. It will accomplish much good for souls. I bless the Legion and your work and I shall pray for its success."

I asked the Nuncio how Matt's Cause was progressing in Rome. He replied "Well. But we need miracles, first-class miracles. That's how you can help in America. Send us ac-

Archbishop Robinson, the Papal Nuncio to Ireland, is in the center; Father Dolan at the left; the Archbishop's secretary at the right.

counts of his miracles when they appear. There are thousands whom he has helped to find work or to keep a pledge, but we need first-class miracles."

I asked how wide-spread devotion to Matt is in Ireland. He answered, "It's growing by leaps and bounds. What gave it its first great lift here in Dublin was the action of Cardinal Verdier at the Eucharistic Congress in 1932. He arrived in Dublin at 6:00, said his Mass and then asked to be taken immediately to Granby Lane and to Matt's home on Rutland Street. That created a great stir and was featured in the newspapers. It had a wide, popular appeal and called the attention of the other prelates, who were here for the Congress, to Matt Talbot's life."

In response to my request, the Archbishop accompanied me outside to meet Father Ronald and be photographed with us.

As we drove jubilantly out of Phoenix Park, I said to Father Ronald, "We have messages for The Matt Talbot Legion from Archbishop McQuaid, from the Papal Nuncio, and from the President of Ireland. We've left out the man who is better known in America than any of these: Premier de Valera. Shouldn't we try to see him also?" Father Ronald said, "And the plane goes tomorrow morning?"

"Yes," I replied, "but maybe we can see him this afternoon. Let's try."

Upon our return to the hotel, I immediately telephoned Mr. Cassidy. "Do you know anyone close to de Valera?"

"I don't know any one too close to him. But I can do my best. You want to see him too? And you're leaving tomorrow? That leaves us only this afternoon. I've heard that appointments with the Premier have to be made at least two weeks in advance. However I'll do my best. I'll call you shortly."

While I was at lunch, he telephoned, "The Premier will give you an appointment Thursday, but until then he hasn't a free minute."

"I'll be home in America on Thursday. Do you think I could accomplish anything by going now to his office?"

"Well, the word is that he hasn't any free time, but I have a feeling that if you went personally. . . . "

"Where's his office, Mr. Cassidy?

"He has two, one in Stephens Green, the other in the Dail. I can find out which he's in if you'll wait."

"I can find out myself just as quickly by going first to the Dail. There's not a minute to lose."

Not waiting to finish lunch, I took a taxi to the Dail, telling the driver to go to the entrance leading to the offices of the Premier. We were soon in sight of the imposing parliamentary buildings of the Dail. Mounting the staircase, I noticed, at its summit, two soldiers on guard, closely observing all visitors. To their left, there was an Information Booth in which an officer presided. I asked him if I could speak for a minute to Premier de Valera's secretary.

He asked, "Does he know you?"

I said "No, just tell him I'm an American priest who is here in Ireland in the interests of an organization, named after a native of Dublin, The Matt Talbot Legion. Tell him please, that my business with him is brief."

The officer asked my name, picked up the phone and delivered my message to Mr. de Valera's secretary. The officer replaced the phone and said, "He'll see you, Father." He pressed a button and in answer a soldier appeared and was told to conduct me to the office of the Premier's secretary.

We mounted a series of majestic staircases, then through a door on which there were in Gaelic the words "The Leader." The soldier led me down a corridor, past a series of offices and into a large waiting room at the end of the corridor. I waited there.

Eamon de Valera, former Prime Minister of Ireland with Father Dolan.

Presently a young, tall, pleasant-faced, rosy-cheeked giant of a man entered, note-book and pencil in hand. I liked the big man on sight.

He asked my name. I said, "My name is Father Dolan, a Carmelite."

"Carmelite,!" he exclaimed. "You're welcome. As a matter of fact, I have just completed the itinerary for Premier de Valera's visit next month to the Jubilee Congress in honor of the Carmelite St. Therese in France." (There she is again, I thought.) We shook hands and I started my plea.

As rapidly as I could talk, I explained my business in Ireland and the reasons why I wanted "just a word with Premier de Valera."

The secretary said, "But, Father, he has just so many minutes in the day, and I'm making appointments now for two weeks hence. I'm telling you the truth when I say that his schedule here (he flipped a page in his note book) simply does not permit a single additional appointment."

"I know. But if, after listening to my one point, you don't agree with me, I'll give up."

He smiled a little and I could see that my persistence rather amused than annoyed him. He told me to go ahead. So I continued, "I bear messages to the members of The Matt Talbot Legion from the Archbishop, from the Papal Nuncio, and from President O'Kelly. Would you or would the Premier want me to return to America without a message from Mr. de Valera too? He's better known in the States than any of these others. To return without a message from him would be to slight him; am I right?"

The twinkle in his eyes grew brighter. He said, "As a matter of fact, the Premier isn't even here at the moment; he's out to lunch."

"Fine. When he returns, he'll have to pass along that corridor out there, won't he? Couldn't you post me there, and I could shake his hand and get a brief word from him to The Legion without disturbing his schedule at all."

The secretary surrendered. He said, "The Premier wouldn't dream of receiving a priest in the corridor, Father. And I don't think that busy as he is, he'd want me to turn away a man as eager as you are to see him. Can you wait?"

"I can wait all afternoon. And while I'm waiting, I'll be thanking you, every inch of you, for your kindness."

He took my name and made a few notes about the purpose of my visit. I then asked his name. It was Seamus McHugo, a grand name for a grand gentleman.

Mr. McHugo went out through the door he had entered to my left. In about ten minutes I heard footsteps in the corridor and voices, and presently Mr. McHugo entered the waiting room through the door to my right. His face bore a broad grin, as leaving the door open, he said, "Father, the Premier will receive you now."

He indicated that I was to pass through the opened door which led into a large office, in which, at a desk at the far end, Premier de Valera was seated. He rose, walked across the room to meet me, shook hands and drew up a chair for me facing him at the side of his desk.

I said, "It is a great honor to be received by the Premier of Ireland."

He replied, "I am always glad to meet friends from America. And especially happy to meet a Carmelite, for I count many Carmelites amongst my closest friends. You are in Dublin in connection with Matt Talbot?"

"Yes, Your Excellency. I suppose you're familiar with his life."

"Not too familiar. I have often resolved to read more about him. My secretary says you wrote the first American life of him. Americans are always brief and businesslike, and so, I suppose, is your book. Would you send me a copy?"

Of course I agreed. Then I explained The Matt Talbot Legion. The Premier commented, "It's a movement that ought to do much good. Naturally I'm pleased that such an organization should have as its patron a workman of Ireland."

"I have told your secretary, Your Excellency, that I have messages to the members of the Legion from everybody that matters except yourself. Would you write a word to them?"

I had my pen ready for him, but he used his own for this message:

May The Matt Talbot Legion in America prosper and achieve the object of their prayers.

(Signed) *Eamon de Valera*

I arose, saying, "I feel that I have taken too much of your time already. I promised your secretary not to detain you."

He rose also and asked "What part of America are you from?"

"From Englewood, New Jersey, although my family home is in Syracuse, not far from your mother's home. Rochester."

He smiled and said, "I always thought that a strange name for an American city, Rochester."

As we shook hands in farewell, he said "Give my regards to my American friends. The best of luck to you and your Matt Talbot Legion. I look forward to reading your life of Matt."

Leaving, I passed up and down the corridor several times seeking Mr. McHugo, who finally emerged, and when I finished thanking him, I felt that I had really succeeded for once in thanking a man adequately. I left the Dail walking on air and feeling that the message from de Valera was a fitting climax to my efforts in Ireland in behalf of The Matt Talbot Legion.

But there was to be a further climax, even more fitting, to terminate the Dublin mission.

At lunch time, I had agreed to meet Father Ronald in Granby Lane at three o'clock, for our final visit with Mrs. Purcell. But the unexpected length of my visit in the Dail caused me to be late. I arrived at Granby Lane at 3:45. I said to Father Ronald, "I saw de Valera and here's his message to the Legion."

Mrs. Purcell was as jubilant as we were. She declared that she was not surprised, because she had been certain both Matt and St. Therese would promote the success of our mission in Dublin.

"You yourself had a lot to do with its success, Mrs. Purcell," I said, "and it is fitting that our last moments in Dublin, like our first moments, should be spent in Granby Lane and with you."

We visited a while, reviewing the activities of our nine days in Dublin, and we laughingly agreed that even if we had nine more days, they could not be used in Matt Talbot work, because there were no more of his relatives or acquaintances to see and no more of his Relics to be had.

Because our plane was to leave early the next morning, I said my last prayer in Granby Lane that evening, and as I rose from my knees at Matt Talbot's Shrine (and this is the further, fitting climax to which I referred), Mrs. Purcell, bidding me farewell, handed me an envelope containing a note, saying, "Please read this on the plane."

Her note read:

The Mission,
Granby Lane, Dublin

Dear Father,

Go, Father, in God's Holy Name, to do the work of God Mary, Therese and Matt in America.

That your Matt Talbot Legion may flourish is my prayer and that of all of Matt's friends, now your friends too, in Dublin.

Tell the sick souls, in "Our Greater Ireland" across the seas, of the great *Doctor* Talbot.

Pray to our Therese for his speedy Canonization. We need Matt in Ireland as you do in America. We will unite our prayers to yours for alcoholics and for all the members of Matt's Legion. Safe journey, dear Father, and good health for the work ahead.

Yours respectfully,

*S. Purcell*

"Go, Father, in God's Holy Name, to do the work of God, Therese and Matt in America. Tell sick souls of the great *Doctor* Talbot." It seems to me, dear readers, that these words of the devout and zealous Mrs. Purcell may well be taken not merely by me but also by you as our slogan for the future. So, as she said to me, I say to you, "Go in God's Holy Name to do the work of Matt Talbot in your various communities and towns, in your offices and homes. Be zealous apostles of The Matt Talbot Legion; bring it to the notice of all you can reach.

"Tell sick souls of the great *Doctor* Talbot. As members of the Legion, pray for those sick souls, the alcoholics of America, privately and publicly, and pray often also for the Canonization of the holy workman, Matt Talbot."

# Supplement

I HAVE assembled here, in the Supplement, items for which there was no suitable place in the body of the book but which nevertheless throw further light on Matt Talbot's life.

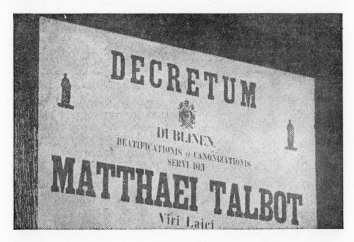

The heading on the Latin Decree, signed by the Holy Father, announcing that the Cause of Matt Talbot's Beatification and Canonization had been officially opened by the Sacred Congregation of Rites. Copies of the Decree were posted on the doors of all the churches of Rome, and in some Dublin churches, in May, 1947.

### Partial Translation of the Holy Father's Decree

"Ireland has deserved for many centuries to be called the Island of Saints and the Nurse of Heroes.

"This Congregation is now considering, with the probable hope of a happy result, the Cause of the workman, Matt Talbot. May God grant that the example of this Servant of God may preserve workmen from the teachings of those who are trying to upset the social order.

"Matthew, the son of Charles Talbot and Elizabeth Bagnal, legitimately married (who had twelve children in their family) was born in a poor quarter in Dublin on the second of May in the year 1856 and was baptised on the fifth of the same month. He passed his boyhood, in great moral innocence, both at home and in the school of the Irish Christian Brothers being led on by the most pious example of his parents and the examples and exhortations of his teachers. At the age of twelve he began manual labour and gradually began to indulge in drunkenness. His parents tried to withdraw him from this vice, but in vain. For fifteen years he continued in this vice and omitted to frequent the sacraments. He did not, however, lose his Faith, nor did he abstain from all religious practices. Never did he offend against chastity.

"It happened that in the year 1884, by a disposition of most loving Divine Providence, one Saturday, being without money through not having worked during the week, he went to the place where his companions were accustomed to congregate for the purpose of drinking. He trusted to be invited by them, but he was disappointed. Detesting such false friendship, moved by Divine Grace, he determined to abandon his evil ways and become good.

"After being reconciled to God by sacramental confession, he took a firm pledge to abstain entirely for three months from all intoxicating drink. Having carried this out faithfully for three months, he renewed his pledge, at first for one year, and then for life, which by conquering himself he observed perfectly up to his death.

"Nor was this sufficient. He began such a form of life that, especially in a workman, can scarcely be conceived. Besides carrying out the duties committed to him, faithfully and with the greatest diligence, he freely undertook corporal penances. He used a bare board for a bed and a log of wood for a pillow. For bedclothes, even in winter-time, he used sacks. He bound his body tightly with iron chains with which he subdued his flesh day and night. He fasted almost the entire year, eating his very small allowances of food on his bended knees.

"Being content with very little sleep, he passed almost the whole night in prayer. He burned with an intense love for Our Lady. Having joined the Third Order of St. Francis he piously observed its laws. In a word, he so exercised all the virtues up to the time of his death, that his companions regarded him as a saintly man.

"On the seventh day of June, 1925 while he was going to hear Mass, he died suddenly.

"After only six years in the Dublin Curia the Informative Process was begun concerning the report of his sanctity, his writings and finally concerning the absence of cult. On the twenty-seventh of November, 1937 this Sacred Congregation published the decree concerning his writings.

"Meanwhile many letters were sent to the Supreme Pontiff by all the Archbishops and Bishops of Ireland, by the President of the Government, by the Apostolic Nuncio, by many Abbots, by the

Provincial Superiors of many Orders and Congregations, by the Lord Mayor of Dublin, by the Trade Unions and by others, asking for the Introduction of his Cause.

"A full report having been made to His Holiness Our Lord Pope Pius XII on the twenty-eighth day of February, 1947, His Holiness agreeing with the Rescript of the Eminent Cardinals deigned to sign with his own hand, the commission for the Introduction of the Cause of the Servant of God, Matthew Talbot."

## MATT'S FAVORITE CHURCHES IN DUBLIN

Father Ronald and I resolved to say a prayer at all the places in Dublin sanctified by Matt's presence. Therefore, besides kneeling at his grave in Glasnevin, at the place of his death in Granby Lane and in his room on Rutland Street, we visited all the churches which Matt habitually frequented. These churches were not few in number. In each of them we said a prayer for the members of The Matt Talbot Legion; in each of them we noticed a statue of St. Therese.

Matt's parish church was St. Joseph's on Berkeley Road, served by secular priests. See photo on Page 53.)

On Page 33 we reproduce the Shrine of St. Therese of Lisieux in the Carmelite Church of St. Theresa on Clarendon Street. Matt gave the first contribution towards the erection of this Shrine of the Little Flower. The Jesuit Church of St. Francis Xavier is shown on Page 53.

The church nearest Martin's Lumber Yard was the Church of St. Lawrence O'Toole, shown on Page 33. After his work Matt visited this church daily "to see Our Lord."

On the second Sunday of the month, Matt went to the Franciscan Church on Merchant's Quay for the monthly Communion of the Third Order of St. Francis. This church is shown on Page 33.

On other Sundays, Matt, in his younger days, went either to St. Francis Xavier's or to the Pro-Cathedral, Marlborough Street. (See photo, Page 33.) In this latter church, Matt was baptized. After his first illness in 1923, he went on Sunday to a church nearer his home, the Dominican Church of St. Saviour, near Granby Lane. He was on his way to St. Saviour's when he dropped dead. St. Saviour's is pictured on Page 124.

Other churches less frequently visited by Matt were the Augustinian Church in John's Lane and the Vincentian Church at Phibsboro (see Page 53). It was to the latter church that Matt went every evening after work in the early months of his conversion to put distance between him and the tavern he had abandoned.

The Tavern itself is shown on Page 70, and on Page 70 there is my photograph taken on the corner of Newcombe Avenue and North Strand, where Matt stood that fateful day when all his drinking companions passed him without inviting him to drink. That evening he took his pledge at Holy Cross Seminary, called also Clonliffe College and pictured on Page 70.

On that Sunday morning, June 7, 1925, when Matt dropped dead in Granby Lane, his fall was seen by Mrs. Anne Keogh, who kept a general store in the Lane. She called her son, Christopher, and both ran over to where he lay. Seeing his condition, she brought some water and lifting his head to give him a drink, she realized that it was not a faintness but that he was dying. As she put the cup of water to his lips, Matt opened his eyes but did not speak. He then laid his head down and as she withdrew her hand from under it, he died.

A fairly large number of the relatives of Mrs. Keogh still live in Granby Lane. Christopher Keogh, present at Matt's death, is now sixty-five and is pictured with me on Page 125. Mrs. Mary Keogh, daughter-in-law of Mrs. Keogh, is shown with me on Page 125. May Keogh, granddaughter of Mrs. Keogh, is pictured with Father Ronald on Page 125.

The picture of Granby Lane on this page shows in the background the Dominican Church of St. Saviour's, whither Matt was bound when he died. In the foreground of the picture, left to right, are Mrs. Anne Keogh, Mrs. Andrews, Christopher Keogh. The two children are May and Joseph Keogh, grandchildren of the old lady.

Granby Lane. In the background looms the Dominican Church of St. Saviour's whither Matt was bound when he died. In the foreground, left to right, are Mrs. Anne Keogh, Mrs. Andrews, Christopher Keogh. The two children are May and Joseph Keogh, grandchildren of the old lady.

*Top left.* Mrs. Mary Keogh, daughter-in-law of Mrs. Anne Keogh, with Father Dolan. See page 124. *Top right.* Father Dolan with Christopher Keogh. See page 124. *Center.* Left to right: Mrs. Purcell; May Keogh, granddaughter of Mrs. Anne Keogh; Mollie Murphy, niece of Mrs. Purcell; Father Ronald. *Right.* Father Dolan with Catherine Carrick. See page 64.

# POEMS IN MEMORY OF MATT TALBOT

MRS. ANNIE SWEENEY, erstwhile custodian of Matt Talbot's Room, who forms the subject of Chapter 13 of this book, possessed two poems, of which she writes, "These are, in my opinion the most beautiful poems concerning holy Matt that have ever been written. Could you publish them?" They are reproduced below.

## MATT TALBOT

### I

Thou gentle soul so holy yet so humble
The struggle of thy earthly life is o'er
Enjoy in glory with God's saints and angels
The promised crown of life for evermore.

### II

Saintly eyes of thine devoutly feasting,
On the vision of the Blessed Trinity,
Wrapt in prayer, ecstatic — contemplating
Heaven's secret now revealed to thee.

### III

Wonder not the world misunderstood thee,
Honored with the gift of perfect prayer,
While on earth men troubled not to know thee
Angels watched thy soul with anxious care.

### IV

Happy death of Dublin's humble workman,
Holy call that set his spirit free,
Man of God, whose life of austere penance
Won a kingdom for eternity.

## THE DEATH OF MATT TALBOT

Granby Lane, a morning in June,
An alley concealed from the traffic way,
A grey church-spire above the gloom
Of streets, asleep at the break of day.

A shadowy form struggling along,
Frail shoulders bent with the weight of years,
A labourer—one of the common throng—
Out of the valley of mist appears.

The delicate features are worn and grey,
The pallor of death is upon the cheek;
The eyes, dull, clouded, scarce see the way
On the path which the senses, accustomed, seek.

Ah, subtle Time! ease your restless hand,
See the twitching muscles, the bending knees;
Stay the course of your running sand
Till the penitent reaches God's House of Ease.

But, futile pleading, remorseless Time,
That silvered the hair, and furrowed the brow,
Severs the links of a life, sublime,
And bids death summon the pilgrim now.

A pain-racked body inert on the road,
A rough stone under the lifeless head,
For the soul is freed of its earthly load,
The penitent labouring man is—dead.

Yet, not alone, for an angel guard,
And companion through years of prayer and pain,
Raises the soul from the dust unscarred,
And smiles, for the vigil was not in vain.

Labourer! Your weakness, your strength, your toil
Have given us courage to hope again;
Have taught men, goaded on earth, to smile
To the Master who sees and assuages pain.

# Methods Used in Ireland to Propagate Devotion to Matt Talbot

IN DUBLIN a group of prominent professional men, who meet weekly at lunch and call themselves The Matt Talbot Circle have as the one purpose of their little organization the distribution of copies of the life of Matt Talbot. They distribute free of charge as many copies as their funds permit and pay for the printing of the leaflet *Make Matt Talbot Known* which they insert in every copy of Matt's "Life" which they distribute. I reprint their leaflet here:

"You can make Matt Talbot known by spreading the story of his life. Here are suggestions. When you have read his Life, pass it on. Give copies to your friends and to those with whom you work. Arrange for distribution at missions and retreats. Send parcels of them to a hospital, a home, or an institution. Leave the booklet behind you in offices, clubs, trains, buses, taxis, waiting rooms of all kinds—everywhere.

"Example is the great teacher. By taking up one or more of these suggestions you will help to radiate the wonderful example of Matt Talbot, so needed by the world to-day — his spirit of prayer and penance, his love of the Mass, his deep sense of justice, his unbounded charity, his zeal for God's glory and the salvation of souls. Moreover, to many a poor sinner, you will bring new hope and courage, for in his early years did not Matt Talbot neglect the duties of his religion and pawn even his boots for a drink?"

# PRAYERS

## PRAYERS TO HELP ALCOHOLICS

### (Official Prayers of The Matt Talbot Legion)

O God, Who resists the proud and gives grace to the humble, grant us true humility, and lift from our hearts all excessive love of the flesh or of earthly things so that living soberly, justly and piously, we may obtain eternal rewards, through Christ, Our Lord. Amen.

O, God Who can justify sinners and does not desire their death, we beseech You to protect with Your help Your servants who trust in You, that they may become and remain Your friends and may not be separated from You by any temptation whatsoever.

In Your mercy, O Lord, when our wills rebel, our wills to Thee compel. Through Christ, Our Lord. Amen.

(Prayers taken from the Missal, Votive Masses ad postulandam humilitatem, et pro tentatis and the Secret of 4th Sunday after Pentecost.)

## PRAYER TO THE PATRONS OF THE LEGION

Come, O Holy Spirit, fill the hearts of Thy faithful, and kindle in them the fire of Thy love.

Refuge of Sinners, pray for us

St. Therese, leading souls back to God, pray for us

St. Therese, Wonder Worker of our own time, pray for us.